my revision notes

OCR A Level

RELIGIOUS STUDIES
RELIGION AND ETHICS

Chris Eyre
Julian Waterfield

HODDER
EDUCATION
AN HACHETTE UK COMPANY

Orders: please contact Bookpoint Ltd, 130 Park Drive, Milton Park, Abingdon, Oxon OX14 4SE. Telephone: (44) 01235 827720. Fax: (44) 01235 400401. Email education@ bookpoint.co.uk Lines are open from 9 a.m. to 5 p.m., Monday to Saturday, with a 24-hour message answering service. You can also order through our website: www.hoddereducation.co.uk

ISBN: 978 1 5104 1805 9

© Chris Eyre and Julian Waterfield 2018

First published in 2018 by

Hodder Education,

An Hachette UK Company

Carmelite House

50 Victoria Embankment

London EC4Y 0DZ

www.hoddereducation.co.uk

Impression number   10 9 8 7 6 5 4 3 2

Year   2022   2021   2020   2019   2018

Cover photo © Lightspring/Shutterstock.com

Typeset by Integra Software Services Pvt. Ltd., Pondicherry, India

Printed in Spain by Graphycems

A catalogue record for this title is available from the British Library.

Get the most from this book

Everyone has to decide his or her own revision strategy, but it is essential to review your work, learn it and test your understanding. These Revision Notes will help you to do that in a planned way, topic by topic. Use this book as the cornerstone of your revision and don't hesitate to write in it – personalise your notes and check your progress by ticking off each section as you revise.

Tick to track your progress

Use the revision planner on pages iv–vi to plan your revision, topic by topic. Tick each box when you have:

- revised and understood a topic
- tested yourself
- practised the 'Now test yourself' questions and checked your answers.

You can also keep track of your revision by ticking off each topic heading in the book. You may find it helpful to add your own notes as you work through each topic.

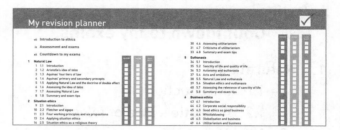

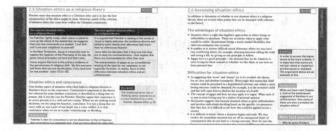

Features to help you succeed

Exam tips and checklists

Expert tips are given throughout the book to help you polish your exam technique in order to maximise your chances in the exam. The exam checklists provide a quick-check bullet list for each topic.

Typical mistakes

The author identifies the typical mistakes candidates make and explains how you can avoid them.

Now test yourself

These short, knowledge-based questions provide the first step in testing your learning. Answers are at the back of the book.

Revision activities

These activities will help you to understand each topic in an interactive way.

Key terms

Clear, concise definitions of essential key words are provided where they first appear.

Key words from the specification are highlighted in bold throughout the book.

Making links

Useful links are provided to other topics within the specification.

Key quotes

Quotes are provided from sources of wisdom or scholars named on the specification to help you understand key concepts.

My revision planner

REVISED   TESTED   EXAM READY

	REVISED	TESTED	EXAM READY

REVISED | TESTED | EXAM READY

Introduction to ethics

What is ethics?

Ethics refers to the branch of philosophy that deals with moral principles, specifically how we act or behave.

Ethics is not the same as study of laws: Murder is morally and legally wrong. Telling a lie in most circumstances is not against the law, but it could be viewed as morally wrong.

Ethics is not the same as customs and culture. There are different customs on how we greet others – a kiss on the cheek or a handshake, yet to fail to shake hands with someone is not usually seen as morally wrong.

Types of ethical questions

There are three main levels of ethical questions.

Meta ethics: From the Greek *meta* meaning above and beyond. The study of the meaning of ethical concepts, e.g. what does 'good' mean? Does it actually exist?

Normative ethics: Considers ethical theories that give advice on how we ought to behave, e.g. utilitarianism, Natural Law

Applied ethics: Discusses specific problems in ethics, e.g. should euthanasia be permitted?

Descriptive ethics: Explores different ethical views that vary across cultures – such as the sociological study of ethics

Approaches to normative ethics

In normative ethics, theories are often characterised as being **absolutist** or **relativist**. An absolutist believes that moral rules are fixed and apply at all times and all places. A relativist believes that moral rules are not fixed but are dependent on situation or culture.

Ethical theories can also be characterised as **deontological** or **teleological**. A deontological ethic concentrates on whether the action itself is good – for example, is it right or wrong to steal?

A teleological ethic judges the rightness of an action by the consequence; it may be acceptable to steal if your family is starving.

As a generalisation:
● Natural Law and Kantian ethics are absolutist and deontological.
● Utilitarianism and situation ethics are relativist and teleological.

> ### Key terms
>
> **Absolutism** In ethics, the idea that right and wrong is fixed at all times and for all people
>
> **Deontological** An ethic that is focused on the rightness or wrongness of the action itself
>
> **Relativism** The idea that what is right or wrong is not fixed but is dependent on situation or culture
>
> **Teleological** The idea that goodness is determined by the outcome of actions

> ### Typical mistake
>
> **A caution on deontological and teleological ethics**
>
> The division of ethical theories into deontological and teleological is a generalisation. It is possible to argue that Natural Law is teleological and that rule utilitarianism is not completely relativist. When thinkers put forward theories on what is right and wrong, they do not plan to be absolutist, relativist, deontological or teleological. They are put into these boxes by others at a later date!

Ethics and religion

A key question in ethics is the relationship between God and ethics. If it is believed that God has revealed commands on how to live, for example, in the Bible or the Qur'an, then it could be argued that these commands are all that are needed and that they must be followed.

The three main views on the relationship between religion and ethics are:

1 **Autonomous**. Ethics is separate to theology and religion. What is right and wrong does not depend on religion at all.
2 **Heteronomous**. Ethics and religion depend on each other.
3 **Theonomous**. Right and wrong is dependent entirely on the command of God. This is sometimes known as Divine Command Ethics.

Enjoy it!

The topics you will come across in Religion and Ethics will give you theories to address some of life's greatest questions and you will look at issues that are current and controversial. Unlike some subjects, there are no easy or agreed answers, so it is important that you are an active student of the course. This means that you don't just passively learn different ideas but that you actually get involved in thinking about each of the topics and which of the ideas you agree with. The best students enjoy their learning and are passionate about RS.

Assessment and exams

How the assessment objectives work depends on whether you are studying Religious Studies for AS- or A-level. If you are doing an AS course then there is no level 6 and the marks are split between AO1 and AO2 evenly. If you are doing an A-level course, then 60% of the marks are for AO2. The difference in weightings does not affect the advice in this book, nor what makes an essay a good essay: you do not have to do anything different at A-level to AS-level, it's just that how good you are at the different skills is given a different number of marks. Equally, don't feel you have to separate out AO1 and

AO2 – write a series of great paragraphs and trust the marker to filter things out!

At AS-level, your exam is 1 hour and 15 minutes and you have to do two questions (from a choice of three). At A-level, your exam is 2 hours and you have to do three questions (from a choice of four). *If you are doing the AS-level, you only need Chapters 1–6 of this book; you will need all nine chapters for the full A-level.* Allowing time for settling down and choosing your questions, you basically have 35 minutes at AS-level and not much more at A-level for an essay. That doesn't seem much, but remember that the examiner will be aware of this.

Assessment objective 1: Knowledge and understanding

You will be able to see here that the marks are gained for being able to choose the right information to help you to answer the question. Better essays come from being more precise and knowing a useful range of material which you can explain concisely. The levels of response mark scheme for AO1 is included below.

Level (Mark)	Levels of response: Assessment objective 1 (AO1)
6 (14–16)	An **excellent** demonstration of knowledge and understanding in response to the question: ● fully comprehends the demands of, and focuses on, the question throughout ● excellent selection of relevant material which is skilfully used ● accurate and highly detailed knowledge which demonstrates deep understanding through a complex and nuanced approach to the material used ● thorough, accurate and precise use of technical terms and vocabulary in context ● extensive range of scholarly views, academic approaches and/or sources of wisdom and authority are used to demonstrate knowledge and understanding
5 (11–13) (AS: 13–15)	A **very good** demonstration of knowledge and understanding in response to the question: ● focuses on the precise question throughout ● very good selection of relevant material which is used appropriately ● accurate, and detailed knowledge which demonstrates very good understanding through either the breadth or depth of material used ● accurate and appropriate use of technical terms and subject vocabulary ● a very good range of scholarly views, academic approaches, and/or sources of wisdom and authority are used to demonstrate knowledge and understanding
4 (8–10) (AS: 10–12)	A **good** demonstration of knowledge and understanding in response to the question: ● addresses the question well ● good selection of relevant material, used appropriately on the whole ● mostly accurate knowledge which demonstrates good understanding of the material used, which should have reasonable amounts of depth or breadth ● mostly accurate and appropriate use of technical terms and subject vocabulary ● a good range of scholarly views, academic approaches and/or sources of wisdom and authority are used to demonstrate knowledge and understanding

Level (Mark)	Levels of response: Assessment objective 1 (AO1)
3 (5–7) (AS: 7–9)	A **satisfactory** demonstration of knowledge and understanding in response to the question: ● generally addresses the question ● mostly sound selection of mostly relevant material ● some accurate knowledge which demonstrates sound understanding through the material used, which might however be lacking in depth or breadth ● generally appropriate use of technical terms and subject vocabulary ● a satisfactory range of scholarly views, academic approaches, and/or sources of wisdom and authority are used to demonstrate knowledge and understanding with only partial success
2 (3–4) (AS: 4–6)	A **basic** demonstration of knowledge and understanding in response to the question: ● might address the general topic rather than the question directly ● limited selection of partially relevant material ● some accurate, but limited, knowledge which demonstrates partial understanding ● some accurate, but limited, use of technical terms and appropriate subject vocabulary ● a limited range of scholarly views, academic approaches and/or sources of wisdom and authority are used to demonstrate knowledge and understanding with little success
1 (1–2) (AS: 1–3)	A **weak** demonstration of knowledge and understanding in response to the question: ● almost completely ignores the question ● very little relevant material selected ● knowledge very limited, demonstrating little understanding ● very little use of technical terms or subject vocabulary ● very little or no use of scholarly views, academic approaches and/or sources of wisdom and authority to demonstrate knowledge and understanding
0 (0)	No creditworthy response

Assessment objective 2: Analysis and evaluation

AO2 is about your ability to argue in response to the question. Examiners are making an assessment of your 'extended response' – how well are you arguing? Can you show that you have thought about a range of different approaches to the issue in the question? Are you critical about all the points you offer? Do you develop the arguments you give rather than stating them and moving on? The levels of response mark scheme for AO2 is included below.

Level (Mark)	Levels of response: Assessment objective 2 (AO2)
6 (21–24)	An **excellent** demonstration of analysis and evaluation in response to the question: ● excellent, clear and successful argument ● confident and insightful critical analysis and detailed evaluation of the issue ● views skilfully and clearly stated, coherently developed and justified ● answers the question set precisely throughout ● thorough, accurate and precise use of technical terms and vocabulary in context ● extensive range of scholarly views, academic approaches and sources of wisdom and authority used to support analysis and evaluation *Assessment of extended response: There is an excellent line of reasoning, well-developed and sustained, which is coherent, relevant and logically structured.*
5 (17–20) (AS: 13–15)	A **very good** demonstration of analysis and evaluation in response to the question: ● clear argument which is mostly successful ● successful and clear analysis and evaluation ● views very well stated, coherently developed and justified ● answers the question set competently ● accurate and appropriate use of technical terms and subject vocabulary ● a very good range of scholarly views, academic approaches and sources of wisdom and authority used to support analysis and evaluation *Assessment of extended response: There is a well-developed and sustained line of reasoning which is coherent, relevant and logically structured.*

Level (Mark)	Levels of response: Assessment objective 2 (AO2)
4 (13–16) (AS: 10–12)	A **good** demonstration of analysis and evaluation in response to the question: ● argument is generally successful and clear ● generally successful analysis and evaluation ● views well stated, with some development and justification ● answers the question set well ● mostly accurate and appropriate use of technical terms and subject vocabulary ● a good range of scholarly views, academic approaches and sources of wisdom and authority are used to support analysis and evaluation *Assessment of extended response: There is a well-developed line of reasoning which is clear, relevant and logically structured.*
3 (9–12) (AS: 7–9)	A **satisfactory** demonstration of analysis and/or evaluation in response to the question: ● some successful argument ● partially successful analysis and evaluation ● views asserted but often not fully justified ● mostly answers the set question ● generally appropriate use of technical terms and subject vocabulary ● a satisfactory range of scholarly views, academic approaches and sources of wisdom and authority are used to support analysis and evaluation with only partial success *Assessment of extended response: There is a line of reasoning presented which is mostly relevant and which has some structure.*
2 (5–8) (AS: 4–6)	A **basic** demonstration of analysis and evaluation in response to the question: ● some argument attempted, not always successful ● little successful analysis and evaluation ● views asserted but with little justification ● only partially answers the question ● some accurate, but limited, use of technical terms and appropriate subject vocabulary ● a limited range of scholarly views, academic approaches and sources of wisdom and authority to support analysis and evaluation with little success *Assessment of extended response: There is a line of reasoning which has some relevance and which is presented with limited structure.*
1 (1–4) (AS: 1–3)	A **weak** demonstration of analysis and evaluation in response to the question: ● very little argument attempted ● very little successful analysis and evaluation ● views asserted with very little justification ● unsuccessful in answering the question ● very little use of technical terms or subject vocabulary ● very little or no use of scholarly views, academic approaches and sources of wisdom and authority to support analysis and evaluation *Assessment of extended response: The information is communicated in a basic/unstructured way.*
0 (0)	No creditworthy response

Assessment and exams

Countdown to my exams

6–8 weeks to go

- Start by looking at the specification available from **www.ocr.org.uk**. Make sure you know exactly what material you need to revise and the style of the examination. Use the revision planner on pages iv–vi to familiarise yourself with the topics.
- Organise your notes, making sure you have covered everything on the specification. The revision planner will help you group your notes into topics.
- Work out a realistic revision plan that will allow you time for relaxation. Set aside days and times for all the subjects that you need to study, and stick to your timetable.
- Set yourself sensible targets. Break your revision down into focused sessions of around 40 minutes, divided by breaks. These Revision Notes organise the basic facts into short, memorable sections to make revising easier.

REVISED ☐

4–6 weeks to go

- Read through the relevant sections of this book and refer to the exam tips, typical mistakes and key terms. Tick off the topics as you feel confident about them. Highlight those topics you find difficult and look at them again in detail.
- Test your understanding of each topic by working through the 'Now test yourself' questions in the book. Look up the answers in the Answers section on pages 82–84.
- Make a note of any problem areas as you revise, and ask your teacher to go over these in class.
- Look at past papers. They are one of the best ways to revise and practise your exam skills. Write or prepare planned answers to the questions in the exam checklists in the book.
- Try different revision methods. For example, you can make notes using mind maps, spider diagrams or flashcards.
- Track your progress using the revision planner and give yourself a reward when you have achieved your target.

REVISED ☐

One week to go

- Try to fit in at least one more timed practice of an entire past paper and seek feedback from your teacher, comparing your work closely with the mark scheme.
- Check the revision planner to make sure you haven't missed out any topics. Brush up on any areas of difficulty by talking them over with a friend or getting help from your teacher.
- Attend any revision classes put on by your teacher. Remember, he or she is an expert at preparing people for examinations.

REVISED ☐

The day before the examination

- Flick through these Revision Notes for useful reminders – for example, the exam tips, typical mistakes and key terms.
- Check the time and place of your examination.
- Make sure you have everything you need – extra pens and pencils, tissues, a watch, bottled water, sweets.
- Allow some time to relax and have an early night to ensure you are fresh and alert for the examination.

REVISED ☐

My exam

Religious Studies: Religion and Ethics

Date: ....

Time: ....

Location: ....

1 Natural Law

1.1 Introduction

The ethical theory of Natural Law suggests that there is an order to the universe and that all things are better when they act according to this order or purpose. Although Natural Law does not have to be seen as a religious theory, its key thinker Thomas Aquinas (1224–1274) proposes a Christian theory of Natural Law which has become its most famous version. This has been interpreted by Catholic Christians through the centuries to be an absolute and deontological ethic, although it can be argued that there is some flexibility in Aquinas' own version.

The specification says

Topic	Content	Key knowledge
Natural Law	Aquinas' Natural Law, including: ● *telos*	Origins of the significant concept of *telos* in Aristotle and its religious development in the writing of Aquinas
	● the four tiers of law	What they are and how they are related: 1 Eternal Law: the principles by which God made and controls the universe and which are only fully known to God 2 Divine Law: the law of God revealed in the Bible, particularly in the Ten Commandments and the Sermon on the Mount 3 Natural Law: the moral law of God within human nature that is discoverable through the use of reason 4 Human Law: the laws of nations
	● the precepts	What they are and how they are related: ● the key precept (do good, avoid evil) ● five primary precepts (preservation of life, ordering of society, worship of God, education of children, reproduction) ● secondary precepts
	Learners should have the opportunity to discuss issues raised by Aquinas' theory of Natural Law, including: ● whether or not Natural Law provides a helpful method of moral decision-making ● whether or not a judgement about something being good, bad, right or wrong can be based on its success or failure in achieving its *telos* ● whether or not the universe as a whole is designed with a *telos*, or human nature has an orientation towards the good ● whether or not the doctrine of double effect can be used to justify an action, such as killing someone as an act of self-defence.	

1.2 Aristotle's idea of *telos*

Aristotle

Aquinas develops a number of his ideas from his reading of Aristotle. Aristotle believed that the universe and everything within it had a **telos**, a purpose or aim. He arrives at this from his theory of the four causes. The *telos* is the final cause. This is easy for us to accept when it comes to everyday objects – for example, the material cause of the chair is 'wood' and its final cause is to provide a comfortable place for us to sit on. Yet as far as Aristotle is concerned, humans, and even actions, have a *telos*.

Aristotle sees the *telos* of human beings as **Eudaimonia**. This is a notoriously difficult word to translate into English. Its main meaning is happiness but not in the sense of pleasure but rather fulfilment and human flourishing. Hence revision for an exam does lead to happiness in this sense even if it doesn't bring pleasure. For Aristotle, Eudaimonia requires a full human life where we not only experience pleasure but we also participate in society and develop academically as philosophers. This is how we achieve our *telos*.

The Stoics

Another source of Natural Law thinking came from the Stoics. Stoicism viewed the world as an ordered place arranged by nature or by the gods in the best way possible. The stoics believed that we had a divine spark within us that enabled us to reason and understand the universe. The path to human happiness and leading a good life was to accept the natural order of things and live according to nature's rules. Stoicism favoured the rational over the emotional. Our modern use of the word stoicism or being stoical is linked to this; we accept what the universe sends our way without complaining.

What does Aquinas draw from these ancient philosophers?

Aquinas draws several key lessons from these ancient thinkers in producing his own theory of Natural Law.
● *Telos* – the idea that humans have a purpose or end.
● Reason – the world is ordered and rational, we have the capacity given by God to understand it.
● Nature – we have a human nature and it is important to do what is 'natural', i.e. what fits with our nature.
These lessons, in addition to Christian ideas taken from the Bible, are key to understanding Aquinas.

> **Key quote**
>
> In the sense of end or 'that for the sake of which' a thing is done, e.g. health is the cause of walking about. ('Why is he walking about?' we say. 'To be healthy', and, having said that, we think we have assigned the cause.)
>
> Aristotle, *Physics*, II,3

> **Making links**
>
> Look at the theory of the four causes in the Philosophy of Religion book in order to remind yourself of this key idea of Aristotle's.

> **Key quote**
>
> True Law is right reason in agreement with nature; it is of universal application, unchanging and everlasting.
>
> Cicero, *On the Republic*

> **Key words**
>
> *Telos* Literally 'end' or 'purpose'. The idea that everything has a purpose or aim
>
> *Eudaimonia* Flourishing and living well, the ultimate end that all actions should lead towards

> **Exam tip**
>
> The mark scheme levels of response ask examiners to make a judgement about how well you use technical terms. Using words like *telos* correctly and in the right context shows the examiner that you are beginning to speak the language of RS as it were.

Now test yourself

1 What does Aristotle believe about *telos*?
2 What does *Eudaimonia* mean?

1.3 Aquinas' four tiers of law

Aquinas' understanding of Natural Law needs to be understood within his ideas that laws are of a four-fold nature. For Aquinas, there are four tiers or levels of law each dependent on the one above. In order of importance, they are Eternal Law, Divine Law, Natural Law and Human Law.

Eternal Law

The Eternal Law is the law as known in the mind of God. In simple terms, it is his knowledge of what is right and wrong. These are moral truths that we at a human level may be unable to fathom. However, God has given us the ability to reason so we may be able imperfectly to work out some of its application to human life.

Divine Law

The Divine Law refers to the law revealed by God through the commands and teachings through revelation, for example in scripture. These include the Ten Commandments and the moral teachings of Jesus in the Sermon on the Mount. It may seem slightly unusual that Aquinas references Divine Law as he primarily believes that law is rational rather than revealed. However, he believes that these laws revealed by God are reasonable; we could work them out.

Natural Law

Natural Law is the moral thinking that we are all able to do whether or not we have had the divine revelation of scripture. All humans have the capacity to consider and work out the moral rules necessary for achieving our purpose. This involves a rational reflection on our human nature and considering how we might 'do good and avoid evil'.

Human Law

Human Laws are the customs and practices of a society. They are devised by governments and by societies. Ideally, it should be based on what we reason from Natural Law. Aquinas argues that laws are only just if they are based on Divine and Natural Law. To break a Human Law that was not based on Divine or Natural Law would be illegal but would not be immoral.

Eternal Law

Divine Law

Natural Law

Human Law

> **Key quote**
>
> Man is bound to obey secular rulers to the extent that the order of justice requires ... if they command unjust things, their subjects are not obliged to obey them.
>
> Aquinas, *Summa Theologica*, II.II Q104 Article 6

Case studies

Laws that were implemented to prevent peaceful protest by civil rights groups in 1960s America could be broken, argued Martin Luther King, as they were 'unjust laws'.	Nazi leaders on trial for war crimes argued that they were just following orders; they were only obeying the law. This was rejected by judges on the grounds that surely 'nature' shows that such laws were morally wrong.

Now test yourself

TESTED

3 How does Natural Law relate to the rules found in the Bible?
4 Why does Aquinas think that it is permissible at times to break a country's laws?

> **Making links**
>
> See Aquinas' view on the relative merits of reason and revelation in the Developments in Christian Thought book, Chapter 3.

1.4 Aquinas' primary and secondary precepts

The main moral rule or precept according to Aquinas is that we should 'do good and avoid evil'. This is known as the *synderesis* rule. All other moral rules are taken from this.

The primary precepts

Aquinas believed that, when we reflect on our *telos* and understand the *synderesis* rule, there are five primary precepts or rules that emerge:

1 **Preservation of life**. Aquinas argues that we are to preserve life. It is evident that life is important, both our own and that of others. It is natural and reasonable for us for a person to be concerned with 'Preserving its own being and … preserving human life'.
2 **To reproduce**. It is also rational to ensure that life continues and this is the main purpose of sexual intercourse.
3 **To learn**, particularly education of the young. Humans are intellectual creatures and it is natural for us to learn.
4 **To live in an ordered society**. We are social beings and it is good to live in an ordered society where it is possible to fulfil our purpose.
5 **To worship God**. To recognise God as the source of life and to live in a way that pleases him.

Aquinas is suggesting that these are some of the key things that human beings are made for. In fulfilling these precepts, we are fulfilling our *telos*. If we reflect on what it means to be human, these are our key aims in life.

Secondary precepts

The primary precepts are not that specific; they are general statements about what is good for humans. Secondary precepts are more specific rules that can be deduced from the primary precepts. For example, given that preservation of life is a primary precept we can deduce that killing a fellow human is wrong. Whereas the primary precepts are fixed, there is some flexibility in the secondary precepts as these are based on how the primary precepts apply in specific circumstances.

While Catholic interpreters of Aquinas have made quite fixed secondary precepts – for example, a rejection of contraception given that the primary precept is reproduction – Aquinas himself never goes this far. For Aquinas, the secondary precepts are possible applications rather than hard and fast rules.

> **Key word**
>
> *Synderesis* The inner principle directing a person towards good and away from evil

> **Key quote**
>
> This is the first precept of law, that 'good is to be done and pursued, and evil is to be avoided'. All other precepts of the Natural Law are based upon this: so that whatever the practical reason naturally apprehends as man's good (or evil) belongs to the precepts of the Natural Law as something to be done or avoided.
>
> Aquinas, *Summa Theologica*, II.1 Q94

> **Key quote**
>
> To the Natural Law belongs everything to which a man is inclined according to his nature.
>
> Aquinas, *Summa Theologica*, II.I Q94

Now test yourself

5 List the five primary precepts.
6 Can you suggest some secondary precepts that may accompany each of the five primary precepts?

1.5 Applying Natural Law and the doctrine of double effect

There are a number of key features of Natural Law that become apparent when the theory is applied to practical issues or hypothetical scenarios.

1 **Sexual ethics**. A man is attracted to his friend's wife. He pursues an affair with her despite the promises he made to his own wife. It is as though on some level he doesn't see the action as wrong.

Key point: Aquinas argues that there are **real and apparent goods**. When someone does something that is morally wrong, it is because they are pursuing an apparent good (his or her own pleasure) rather than a real good. Aquinas suggests that moral mistakes are reasoning errors. The adulterer really does think the affair is good but has reasoned badly.

2 **Antigone**. The heroine of the play, Antigone, defied the order of King Creon who forbade the burial of her recently deceased brother. She argues that such an order defies the Natural Law of proper burial.

Key point: This shows two other key features of Natural Law. It is a rational system of decision making. Aquinas believes, similarly to Aristotle, that there are intellectual virtues such as prudence – the ability to make sound practical moral decisions. This moral reasoning is something that we can develop and improve. Education really is the answer! Second, it appeals to human nature by claiming that there are certain things which are natural to human beings regardless of time, place or culture. This natural order that Antigone is respecting is 'built in' to the universe.

3 **Euthanasia**. A doctor attempts to treat a terminally ill patient by giving a dose of pain killer with the intention of relieving pain. Ultimately, the pain killer causes the death of the patient. However, this was an unintended, although not unforeseen, consequence of the action so according to Natural Law, the doctor has done nothing wrong. For Natural Law, this would not be euthanasia as the doctor does not intend to end the life of the patient.

Key point: This is the **doctrine of double effect**. Some actions are complex and produce several effects, some good and some bad. For Aquinas, what matters is which effect is intended. He uses the example of self-defence. If you were to fight off an attacker and save your own life (good effect) but the attacker when pushed away hits his head and dies (bad effect), then you are not guilty of doing anything wrong. Your intention is what matters.

4 **Abortion**. As a result of routine tests during pregnancy a woman discovers that the foetus she is carrying is likely to be severely disabled. Her friends suggest to her that she ought to have an abortion as the child is likely to have a very poor quality of life. However, she is a devout Catholic and follows Natural Law thinking. She argues that an abortion would go against the principle of sanctity of life.

Key point: Natural Law ethics prioritises the sanctity of life rather than the quality of life. Whereas a utilitarian or a situation ethicist weighs up the pros and cons of intervention, Natural Law upholds the value of all life.

> **Key quote**
>
> Nothing hinders one act from having two effects, only one of which is intended ... Accordingly the act of self-defence may have two effects: one the saving of one's life; the other, the slaying of the aggressor ... Therefore this act, since one's intention is to save one's life, is not unlawful.
>
> Aquinas, *Summa Theologica*, II.II Q64

Now test yourself

7 What is the doctrine of double effect? Explain with an example.

1.6 Assessing the idea of *telos*

Strengths of Natural Law

- Like other theories which can be seen as absolutist, Natural Law offers clarity and firm moral principles.
- The primary precepts are mostly agreed upon as desirable goods in human life. Reflection on the natural world suggests that these are things that most humans pursue.
- One possible strength of Natural Law is that it is not as rigid and absolutist as it might first appear. The secondary precepts are intended to be reasoned within the context of a society and thus there is some flexibility based on time and place.
- Natural Law values life and values rights. The version of Natural Law put forward by Hugo Grotius (a seventeenth-century Dutch thinker) develops the idea that certain 'rights' for individuals are evident when looking at nature. Unlike theories of **consequentialism**, Natural Law holds that life is intrinsically valuable regardless of its usefulness.

Issues with the idea of *telos*

- Natural Law may be wrong to assume that there is a universal *telos* for human beings: I may wish to prioritise my career at the expense of reproduction, I may live a solitary life of meditation rather than in 'an ordered society', I may not believe that there is a God let alone desire to worship one.
- Linked to this is the idea that *telos* is natural. If natural means in accordance with our nature, then a gay person might be right to claim that homosexuality is natural to them (hence no reproduction) and that it is heterosexuality that is unnatural. Yet if individuals had different *telos* then there is no reason to suppose that there is just one way of life that is natural.
- Natural Law commits the **naturalistic fallacy**. It is guilty of observing what commonly happens in nature and then arguing that this is what must happen. This would be like observing the shape of human teeth, that they are well designed for eating meat, and then claiming that it was morally wrong just to eat vegetables.
- Perhaps the biggest issue with the idea of *telos* is that there may not be a *telos* or purpose at all. Proponents of **existentialism**, such as Jean Paul Sartre (1905–1980), argue that there is no ultimate purpose to human life. Unlike objects which have a maker who plans their purpose before they are made, we exist first and then we are free to choose whatever purposes we see fit, if at all. For Sartre, if atheism is true then there can be no ultimate purpose.
- Hence linked to the above point, it would seem that the idea of *telos* is linked to the idea of a creator God. If there is no God, there can be no *telos*.

Key words

Consequentialism The idea that right and wrong are based on the outcome or consequences of actions

Naturalistic fallacy The idea that it is a mistake to define moral terms with reference to other non-moral or natural terms

Existentialism A school of philosophy that begins with human existence rather than human essence, it argues that humans are free and don't have a fixed nature

Now test yourself

8 Suggest two criticisms of the idea that we have a *telos*.

1.7 Assessing Natural Law

In addition to the issues surrounding the idea of *telos*, there are a number of other issues to consider when examining Natural Law.

Discussing Natural Law

- The focus on 'law' and working out rules which are at the heart of this system is overly legalistic. It means that in some circumstances humanity and respect for people are lost.
- Natural Law may be seen to be a little outdated. Society has moved on and more legalistic interpretations particularly around homosexuality and contraception, both of which prevent reproduction, seem out of step with the modern world.
- Aquinas' view of real and apparent goods could be seen as a little naive. Some humans knowingly commit evil actions, and suggesting they are merely pursuing apparent goods is mistaken. A glance at the day's news suggests that not all humans have a natural inclination towards the good.

Developing arguments on Natural Law

In order to access the higher levels of the mark scheme, points need to be discussed rather than just raised or stated. See the examples below.

Possible strengths of Natural Law	Response/counter-argument
Natural Law claims to have the best of both worlds in that it offers clear and fixed principles as seen in the primary precepts yet also promises that there is flexibility in how these principles might be applied to different circumstances when secondary precepts are formed.	It is not clear that both these things can be the case. Certainly there is a tension between the idea that Natural Law is 'universal in its precepts' (Catechism 1956) and 'application of the Natural Law varies greatly' (Catechism 1957).
Following on from the issue above is the idea of double effect. This seems to allow the flexibility suggested above by allowing both good and bad effects provided the good one is intended.	However, there is a difficulty in judging the intention of a person. It may appear that someone was acting in self-defence and that their attacker's death was an accident but only they will ever know.
One attraction of Natural Law is its reliance on reasoning. It treats humans as mature people who are able to be rational and reflect on moral problems.	This can be challenged in a number of ways. Some thinkers have worried that relying on reason means that the role of scripture is reduced (although Natural Law thinkers would argue there isn't necessarily disagreement between the two). A further challenge to the role of reason comes from the teaching of Augustine that humans are fallen and incapable of reasoning clearly.
Although Natural Law is a religious ethical theory, it is argued by Grotius that belief in Natural Law does not require belief in God. The laws themselves are obvious to reason and can be worked out without God.	It is difficult to accept this for Aquinas' version where one of the precepts is to worship God and there is a reliance on Divine Law. Even Grotius accepts that the answer to why we should follow the law relates back to God.

> **Revision activity**
>
> Use the information on this and the previous page to produce a mind map assessing the Natural Law theory.

1.8 Summary and exam tips

Exam checklist

- Explain Aristotle's idea of *telos* and how Aquinas develops this concept.
- Explain Aquinas' views on the four tiers or levels of law.
- Explain Aquinas' ideas on primary and secondary precepts.
- Assess whether Natural Law enables good moral decisions to be made.
- Consider whether *telos* can be used to decide whether something is good or bad.
- Consider whether the universe has *telos* and whether humans have an orientation towards good.
- Assess whether the idea of double effect is helpful.

Sample work

Although exam questions demand both AO1 and AO2, the conclusion of the essay needs to be written in terms of AO2 – analysis and evaluation. Ask yourself what your essay has argued. This should be the focus of your conclusion. Look at the example and commentary below.

Basic conclusion	Better conclusion
In conclusion, there are some strengths to Natural Law and there are also some weaknesses. So it is difficult to know whether Natural Law is a good ethical theory or not.	While there are some advantages to Natural Law, such as the valuing of human rights, these are not sufficient to suggest that this is a strong theory overall. The key weakness is that it is inflexible to different situations – it would treat both the rape victim and the person who forgot contraception alike in the issue of abortion. This means that rights are not ultimately respected; so the theory is inadequate overall.

Going further: Hugo Grotius and John Finnis

Hugo Grotius (1583–1645) was a Dutch legal philosopher who argued that Natural Law would still apply even if there were not a God. In reality, though, he did believe in God and thought that because nature was God's creation, Natural Law and Biblical law could not contradict each other. He argued that there should be international law based on Natural Law that governed how nations treated each other. He made significant contributions in developing Aquinas' Just War Theory, including identifying some of the circumstances where war may be permissible.

John Finnis (1940–), a modern legal philosopher, has an approach to Natural Law that is based more on Aristotle than Aquinas. Finnis believes that things such as life, knowledge, play, work, aesthetic experience, friendship, practical reasonableness and religion/spirituality are 'basic forms of human flourishing'. If we assume that these are goods to be pursued then these aims, especially the use of practical reason, enable us to suggest certain requirements that humans need. These include the pursuit of basic goods for all, a sense of planning or purpose to life, the idea of a common good for a community, and acting according to conscience. It is from these requirements that moral principles can be drawn such as obeying the law or not torturing others. This allows for a more modern version of Natural Law that is more flexible than some Catholic interpreters of Aquinas.

> **Exam tip**
>
> One way of showing a high level understanding of Natural Law is to show awareness of more modern theories that are a contrast to Aquinas.

2 Situation ethics

2.1 Introduction

Situation ethics is a Christian ethic, but is a very different type of Christian ethic to Natural Law ethics. Its main thinker, Joseph Fletcher (1905–1991), put forward a teleological ethical theory which suggests that, in any situation, the best thing to do is whatever leads to the most loving outcome. He argues that this 'agape' love was what Jesus taught in the New Testament. What is most loving will, of course, vary depending on the situation (hence the name of the theory). This makes situation ethics a relativist ethical theory.

The specification says

Topic	Content	Key knowledge
Situation ethics	Fletcher's situation ethics, including:	
	● agape	Origins of agape in the New Testament and its religious development in the writing of Fletcher
	● the six propositions	What they are and how they give rise to the theory of situation ethics and its approach to moral decision-making: 1 Love is the only thing that is intrinsically good 2 Love is the ruling norm in ethical decision-making and replaces all laws 3 Love and justice are the same thing – justice is love that is distributed 4 Love wills the neighbour's good regardless of whether the neighbour is liked or not 5 Love is the goal or end of the act and that justifies any means to achieve that goal 6 Love decides on each situation as it arises without a set of laws to guide it
	● the four working principles	What they are and how they are intended to be applied: 1 Pragmatism: it is based on experience rather than on theory 2 Relativism: it is based on making the absolute laws of Christian ethics relative 3 Positivism: it begins with belief in the reality and importance of love 4 Personalism: persons, not laws or anything else, are at the centre of situation ethics
	● conscience	What conscience is and what it is not according to Fletcher, i.e. a verb not a noun; a term that describes attempts to make decisions creatively
	Learners should have the opportunity to discuss issues raised by Fletcher's theory of situation ethics, including: ● whether or not situation ethics provides a helpful method of moral decision-making ● whether or not an ethical judgement about something being good, bad, right or wrong can be based on the extent to which, in any given situation, agape is best served ● whether Fletcher's understanding of agape is really religious or whether it means nothing more than wanting the best for the person involved in a given situation ● whether or not the rejection of absolute rules by situation ethics makes moral decision-making entirely individualistic and subjective.		

2.2 Fletcher and agape

The key idea of Joseph Fletcher's ethics is the Greek word *agape,* which translates as 'love'. It is the word used in the New Testament by Jesus when he summarises the commandments as the duty to love God and to love one's neighbour.

For Fletcher, **agape** is the key to situation ethics. Christianity is based on love both in terms of God's love for creation and the command that people love their neighbours. In taking this view, Fletcher is partly drawing on previous writers, such as William Temple, who had argued for an ethic based on love.

Joseph Fletcher dedicates his 1966 book *Situation Ethics* to the taxi driver his friend met in St Louis. The taxi driver came from a long line of Republican voters, but reflected that he would be voting Democrat in the upcoming election as he needed to put his principles aside and do the right thing.

Key quotes

There is only one ultimate and invariable duty, and its formula is 'Thou shalt love thy neighbour as thyself.'
William Temple, *Mens Creatix*

Christian situation ethics has only one … principle or law that is binding and unexceptionable, always good and right regardless of the circumstances. That is 'love' – the agape of the summary commandment to love God and the neighbour.
Fletcher, *Situation Ethics*, p. 30

Key quote

There are times when a man has to push his principles aside and do the right thing.
St Louis taxi driver quoted in Fletcher's *Situation Ethics*

Key words

Agape Unconditional love

Legalism The idea that ethical decision making is by a system of laws

Antinomianism Literally meaning to have no laws at all (Greek *nomos* = law)

Agape versus legalism and antinomianism

Fletcher argues that there are three different approaches to ethics. His favoured approach, situationism, attempts to make a middle way between what he sees as two main errors in ethical thinking: **legalism** and **antinomianism**.

Legalism	Situationism	Antinomianism
Legalism is an overreliance on rules. By the time of Jesus, the Pharisees had 613 specific rules or precepts to uphold. Fletcher argues that Natural Law is also guilty of excessive legalism. Protestants who take the Bible literally are no better.	Situationism is for Fletcher the right approach between the two extremes. This involves taking the principles of your community and using them to 'illuminate' situations. For Fletcher, this means knowing when to apply the principle and when to recognise exceptions. Like tactics in a game, the expert player knows when to ignore the general rule. They know what *agape* (love) requires in that situation.	The word 'antinomianism' literally means 'no laws'. Antinomians believe in freedom to act as one sees fit in any circumstance. Some Christians may claim to act 'as the spirit leads'. Yet to have no rules at all leads to anarchy as we do not know what to do from one situation to the next.

Now test yourself
TESTED

1 Fletcher uses the word 'agape' to describe love. What type of love is this?
2 Agape is a midpoint according to Fletcher. What two things are at either end of the spectrum?

2.3 Four working principles and six propositions

Fletcher argues that the key to understanding the idea of situation ethics is in the six main propositions below, but he starts his account by exploring four principles or assumptions that situation ethics makes.

The four working principles of situationism

1. **Pragmatism**: The question 'What will work?' is more important than the question 'What is true?'. Fletcher does not want theoretical solutions; he requires that a solution works in practice. Thus situation ethics is grounded in experience not theory.

2. **Relativism**: Love is the absolute, everything else is relative to it. Hence the method of situation ethics involves relativism. Although 'love' is the 'why' of our action, the 'how' is contingent and changes. Fletcher argues that the situationist avoids words like 'never' and 'perfect' and 'always' and 'complete' as he avoids the plague, as he avoids 'absolutely'.

3. **Positivism**: We cannot look at the world and discover moral laws, as Natural Law thinks. Values are decided by starting with faith in God and 'positively' reasoning what this might mean in each situation. We create the 'good' rather than discovering it. We decide our values by looking at the situation.

4. **Personalism**: People are the ultimate moral value. Ethics is about human relations yet the legalist is only concerned with laws and rules. Situation ethics says that everything is related to the good of persons. 'Love is of people, by people and for people. Things are to be used; people are to be loved' (Fletcher, *Situation ethics*, page 51).

> **Key word**
>
> **Pragmatism** A philosophical idea that suggests 'truth' should be understood in terms of what works

Now test yourself

3 What are Fletcher's four working principles or assumptions that underpin situation ethics?

> **Making links**
>
> Dietrich Bonhoeffer also argued that ethical decision-making based on love had to be understood relative to the situation. See the Developments in Christian Thought book, Chapter 6.

Fletcher's six propositions in detail

The main body of Fletcher's situation ethics covers six key ideas or propositions that he believes are essential to situation ethics:

1. *Only one thing is intrinsically good, namely love: nothing else at all.* Some things are extrinsically good – they are good because they serve some end, e.g. walking is good because we aim to be healthy. Other things are good in themselves, they are intrinsically good. Only love is truly good in itself.

2. *The ruling norm of Christian decision is love, nothing else.* In the New Testament, Jesus consistently replaces the Old Testament laws with the principle of love, for example by healing someone (hence working) on the Sabbath. Where law and love conflict, we must follow love. Fletcher reminds us that Jesus summed up the whole of Jewish law as 'Love God' and 'Love your Neighbour'.

3. *Love and justice are the same, for justice is love distributed, nothing else.* Justice and love are not opposites or in tension as is often thought (whereby justice might want to see a criminal punished, but love may urge forgiveness). Justice is Christian love being applied rationally and in a calculated manner. Fletcher suggests that this is not a sentimental love, but is the calculation made by businessmen, generals or doctors in deciding who benefits the most.

4. *Love wills the neighbour good whether we like him or not.* Love is an attitude not a feeling; we are dealing with agape not eros. Agape love is selfless and is not necessarily reciprocal. It does not necessarily require anything in return. It is not sentimental. The neighbour can be anyone we come across (as illustrated in the parable of the Good Samaritan). Fletcher notes that Jesus' command to love even extends to loving our enemies (Matthew 5: 43–48).

5. *Only the end justifies the means, nothing else.* Fletcher is not suggesting that any end is justified by any means, but that any loving end is justified by any means. It is whether the end is worthwhile that determines whether the action is worthwhile. Fletcher uses the example of the Second World War resistance fighters who routinely lied and even killed members of their own side because of the importance of their cause.

6. *Love's decisions are made situationally, not prescriptively.* Love is the norm but it doesn't tell us what to do in a specific situation. We have to gather the facts rather than decide the case before we know the facts. One particular issue is sexual ethics where he argues that Christianity has become overly obsessed with rules at the expense of deciding on a situational basis; Fletcher does not answer the question as to whether adultery is wrong; he replies, 'Give me a real case'.

Typical mistake

One common over-simplification of situation ethics involves assuming that loving others is merely being nice to them or being a pushover. This is not how Fletcher sees love. For Fletcher, agape love may involve 'tough love' and making difficult decisions to secure more loving outcomes.

Now test yourself

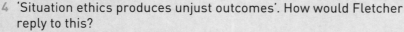
TESTED

4 'Situation ethics produces unjust outcomes'. How would Fletcher reply to this?

5 When asked whether adultery is right or wrong, Fletcher says, 'Give me a real case'. Why does he give this answer?

2.4 Applying situation ethics

Fletcher's book contains a number of cases that he uses to illustrate aspects of his theory.

1 **Abortion after rape**. In 1962 (before abortion was legalised in America), a young patient at a psychiatric unit became pregnant after being raped by a fellow patient. The patient's father requested an abortion take place. The doctors refused on the grounds that abortion was only permitted when the mother's life was in danger.

   Key point: Fletcher suggests this is the wrong outcome. This illustrates how legalism can make the wrong decision. Situation ethics is **person centred** not legalistic.

2 **Sacrificial suicide/euthanasia**. A terminally ill man is offered expensive medical treatment that will prolong his life for a few extra months. It will probably keep him alive long enough for his medical insurance to run out, so his family would not benefit when he dies. If he refuses the medication and dies before the insurance runs out, his family will receive a generous sum.

   Key point: Situation ethics is a **teleological** ethical theory. What makes an action right is that it leads to a good outcome. Fletcher is a pragmatist; it is more important that a course of action works rather than is right. Hence, in this case, it may be permissible to break the normal moral rule and refuse treatment.

3 **Sexual ethics – adultery**. A German woman, Mrs Bergmeier, was in a Russian prisoner of war camp; she became aware that her family were alive in Germany and looking for her. However, the only way someone could obtain release from the camp was through pregnancy; she would then be returned to Germany as a liability. She persuaded a friendly camp guard to help her become pregnant. Upon return to her family, they welcomed her and her child with open arms.

   Key point: Situation ethics is a **relativist** theory; what is right or wrong depends on the situation. We should avoid words such as 'always' and 'never'. Fletcher requested 'give me a real case' when discussing whether adultery was morally right. In the circumstances suggested above, situation ethics would argue that adultery was morally justified and was the most loving thing.

4 **Sexual ethics – prostitution**. A female government agent is asked by her superiors to seduce an enemy spy in order to obtain important information. She said that she was unsure as to whether she could compromise her integrity in this way. She was told although they would not pressurise her to do this it was similar to her brother's role in fighting on the front line risking his life. Given that the information she would get could shorten the war and save many lives, what should she do?

   Key point: What is interesting about the above dilemma is that Fletcher does not suggest an answer. He has given us a method that will help us to decide for ourselves. It is left to the young woman's conscience. For Fletcher, conscience is a verb not a noun (see page 14).

2.5 Situation ethics as a religious theory

Fletcher states that situation ethics is a Christian ethic and is in fact the best interpretation of the ethics taught by Jesus. However, much of the criticism of situation ethics has come from within the Christian community.

The case for situation ethics as a religious theory	The case against situation ethics as a religious theory
As Fletcher rightly notes, when Jesus is asked to sum up the whole of the Jewish law, he suggests that only two commands are needed: 'Love God' and 'Love your neighbour as yourself.'	It is argued that Fletcher's reading of the words of Jesus is highly selective. He condemns divorce and adultery quite clearly and references hell more than he references heaven!
In the New Testament, Jesus is frequently seen to oppose the legalism of the Pharisees of his day. He gives moral principles not hard and fast rules.	Jesus tells his disciples that if they love him they are to obey his commandments – that implies that there are commandments other than love.
Jesus argues that love is the primary evidence of the genuineness of religious faith. 'By this everyone will know that you are my disciples, if you have love for one another' (John 13:34–35).	The interpretation of agape as an unconditional wishing of the best for our neighbour is not explicitly Christian. In reality, there is little difference between situation ethics and act utilitarianism.

Situation ethics and conscience

One further aspect of situation ethics that links to religious theories is Fletcher's focus on the conscience. Conscience is important to the theory but whereas for some thinkers conscience is described as a thing that we possess, this is not the case for Fletcher. Fletcher argues that conscience is an active process; it is a verb and not a noun. When we are making moral decisions, we are using the function, conscience. It is not a thing that we carry with us, nor a part of our mind, nor a voice within. It is only conscience when we are in a sense 'consciencing' or deciding.

> **Key quote**
>
> The traditional error lies in thinking about conscience as a noun instead of as a verb.
> Fletcher, *Situation Ethics*, p. 53

Making links

Fletcher's view on conscience is not too dissimilar to that of Aquinas that conscience is a reasoning tool. Find out more about his view later in this book.

Case study

The atomic bomb

Fletcher ends his book with a case study of the first atomic bombs dropped on Hiroshima and Nagasaki in 1945. Over 150,000 people were killed and even more than this were to die of their injuries in the months and years that followed. US President Truman had appointed a committee to decide on whether to use this new weapon. Most of his military advisors favoured using it as it would shorten the war by years. The scientific advisors were split but were unable to offer other alternatives. Japan surrendered immediately after the bombs were dropped.

Fletcher leaves this case open ended. According to his theory, what would be the right thing to do?

Now test yourself

6 Why does Fletcher believe situation ethics is a religious theory? Why might others disagree with him?

2.6 Assessing situation ethics

REVISED

In addition to discussion of whether or not situation ethics is a religious theory, there are several other points that can be discussed with reference to the theory.

The advantages of situation ethics

- Situation ethics is right that legalistic approaches to ethics brings an inflexibility to situations. There are occasions when to apply rules would be unfair. Situationism brings a much needed flexibility that takes circumstances into account.
- It enables us to answer difficult moral dilemmas where we may have two conflicting duties, for example, choosing between telling the truth and saving a life, by giving us one principle to follow.
- Agape love is a good principle – the demand that we do whatever is most loving for those around us whether we like them or not saves us from personal bias.

Difficulties for situation ethics

- In suggesting that 'never' and 'always' are to be avoided, the theory has no clear and absolute boundaries. Worryingly this means that child torture could be permitted in a hypothetical extreme case where a more loving outcome could be obtained; for example, it is the terrorist's child and this will cause him to disclose the location of a bomb.
- The concept of agape and how we may apply it is vague. What each of us sees as most loving may be a matter of personal opinion.
- McQuarrie suggests that because situation ethics is quite individualistic and involves individuals deciding based on the specific circumstances that they face, it is difficult to see how this could be applied across a society.
- It is difficult to know where a situation begins and ends. We may resolve the immediate situation but set off an unexpected chain of consequences that do not lead to a loving outcome. How far into the future are we required to calculate the outcome? What exactly are we morally responsible for?
- Some thinkers have argued that in reality situation ethics is no different to utilitarianism. This may or may not be a disadvantage depending on what you wish to argue.

Exam tip

In order to access the higher levels of the mark scheme, it is important that points are not just raised or stated but are discussed or analysed. The arguments below are an example of this.

Making links

When you have read Chapter 4, look at the weaknesses suggested of Bentham's act utilitarianism. How many of these are also a problem for situation ethics?

Now test yourself

7 Why do some thinkers argue that situation ethics is similar to utilitarianism?

TESTED

Developing arguments on situation ethics

Proposed strength of situation ethics	Response/counter-argument
Situation ethics is person centred. Whereas legalistic systems such as Natural Law focus on obedience to rules, situation ethics starts with the question of what will work for and be of benefit to the persons involved.	However, the focus on there being no absolutes means that there can be no real idea of 'rights' in situation ethics. This means that in some situations, some persons will be disregarded for the greater good.
Situation ethics gives humans the moral responsibility for the decisions they make. We are not given rules, we are asked to reason about how love should be applied. The idea that conscience is a verb not a noun develops this.	While it may seem good in theory that the power is given to the person making the decision, it is wrong to assume that we all have sufficient expertise to reason on the best outcome, particularly as the idea of agape is hard to apply in some cases.

2.7 Summary and exam tips

Exam checklist

- Explain Fletcher's understanding of agape.
- Explain Fletcher's six propositions that he uses to explain situation ethics.
- Explain Fletcher's four working principles: pragmatism, relativism, positivism and personalism.
- Explain Fletcher's understanding of conscience as a verb not a noun.
- Assess whether situation ethics is a useful means of making moral decisions.
- Assess the extent to which Fletcher's theory of agape is genuinely a religious theory.
- Consider the criticism that situation ethics is individualistic and subjective.

Sample work

To ensure that you get good marks for AO1, it is important that explanations of concepts are clear and detailed. This may involve defining terms and giving examples to show that the term is understood.

Basic explanation	Better explanation
Situation ethics is a moral theory put forward by Joseph Fletcher (1905–1991), who was an American minister who lost his faith in later life. He said that situation ethics was between legalism and antinomianism. He argued that in a moral dilemma we ought to do the most loving thing.	Situation ethics is seen by its founder, Joseph Fletcher, as a middle position between legalism, the excessive reliance on laws such as seen in the approach of the Pharisees, and antinomianism, the belief that no rules at all are required. Fletcher argued that the one principle needed was agape love, an unconditional love. In all moral dilemmas, our one principle should be that we do that which leads to the most loving outcome.

Going further: C.S. Lewis and *The Four Loves*

Joseph Fletcher identified the key principle of Christian moral decision making as agape love.

The author C.S. Lewis noted in his 1960 book, *The Four Loves*, that there are four different Greek words for the idea of love. These are summarised in the table.

Love	Meaning
Storge	A fondness often based on family connection
Philia	A close friendship or companionship
Eros	A sexual love
Agape	Charity, unconditional love, the greatest of all the 'loves'

For Lewis, agape is the greatest of the loves. It is a specifically Christian love and it exists regardless of circumstances. It is not within humanity's natural abilities to practise agape but with God's help it is possible to love God and our neighbours.

Revision activity

One useful activity to show that you understand how the exam works is to try to write your own exam questions. Look at the specification for this topic on page 9 and try to write a possible question that would test both AO1 and AO2. See pages ix–xi for an explanation of what these objectives involve.

3 Kantian ethics

3.1 Introduction

Kantian ethics, as the name suggests, is linked to the moral philosophy of Immanuel Kant (1724–1804). Kant believed that there were absolute moral rules that could be worked out rationally; these moral rules apply in all situations. His ethical theory is absolutist and, unlike other rule-based systems, does not rely directly upon belief in God. Kant's approach is deontological as opposed to teleological; he is interested in right actions rather than right outcomes. The rules that he believed we should follow are called 'categorical imperatives': they are things that we could make into universal laws, they allow us to treat persons as ends (with respect) and would be permissible in a perfect kingdom of ends.

The specification says

Topic	Content	Key knowledge
Kantian ethics	Duty	Origins of the concept of duty (acting morally according to the good regardless of consequences) in deontological and absolutist approaches to ethics
	The hypothetical imperative	What it is (a command to act to achieve a desired result) and why it is not the imperative of morality
	The categorical imperative and its three formulations	What it is (a command to act that is good in itself regardless of consequences) and why it is the imperative of morality based on: 1 Formula of the law of nature (whereby a maxim can be established as a universal law) 2 Formula of the end in itself (whereby people are treated as ends in themselves and not means to an end) 3 Formula of the kingdom of ends (whereby a society of rationality is established in which people treat each other as ends and not means)
	The three postulates	What they are and why in obeying a moral command they are being accepted: 1 Freedom 2 Immortality 3 God
	Learners should have the opportunity to discuss issues raised by Kant's approach to ethics, including: ● whether or not Kantian ethics provides a helpful method of moral decision-making ● whether or not an ethical judgement about something being good, bad, right or wrong can be based on the extent to which duty is best served ● whether or not Kantian ethics is too abstract to be applicable to practical moral decision-making ● whether or not Kantian ethics is so reliant on reason that it unduly rejects the importance of other factors, such as sympathy, empathy and love in moral decision-making.	

Now test yourself

1 Which of the following words can be applied to Kantian ethics: absolutist, relativist, deontological, teleological, religious, secular?

3.2 Kant and duty

Good will

For Kant, the only truly good thing is a **good will** – having good intentions. He famously says that 'good will shines like a precious jewel'. All other things such as courage or wealth may or may not be good dependent on the situation. Kant argues that it doesn't matter if we are prevented from carrying out our intentions; what matters is that we aim to do the right thing. This good will is the desire to do 'duty for duty's sake'.

Duty

If we have a 'good will', we will perform the right action for the right reason. For Kant, the motive and the outward action must correspond. In order to see what **duty** is, it is worth looking at two things that Kant says duty is not:

1 Doing the right thing out of self-interest or because of possible consequences is not duty. A shopkeeper who charges customers fairly just because he figures it is good for business is not doing his duty.
2 Doing the right thing out of inclination (because we feel like it) is not duty. We may feel moved to give to charity one day but not the next. So inclination is a poor guide to what we should or shouldn't do.

Hence, duty is that which we rationally work out that we ought to do. Our emotions and possible consequences are irrelevant. One way to understand this is to think of a profession where there are duties, such as a policewoman. It is her duty to intervene when she sees a crime committed regardless of whether she thinks she will succeed in catching the criminal or whether she feels like it. It is her duty to intervene just because she is a policewoman. Kant believes that all human beings have moral duties that they must act upon just because they are human beings.

> **Key words**
>
> **Good will** The only truly intrinsically good thing, having good motives and intentions
>
> **Duty** The action that is morally required

> **Key quote**
>
> Two things fill the mind with ever new and increasing admiration and reverence ... the starry heavens above me and the moral law within me.
>
> Kant, *Critique of Pure Reason*

Now test yourself

2 What does Kant mean in saying that we should be motivated by duty?

3.3 Hypothetical and categorical imperatives

Kant believes that there are absolute moral duties but how do we work out what they are? A key factor to note in Kantian ethics is the principle of **autonomy**. He believes that human beings have rationality and, unlike other ethical theories, we are able to work out what these rules are. They are not imposed by God or a similar authority. Kant argues that whenever we carry out an action, we are acting upon a **maxim**; in other words there is a rule that we have in mind that we are following. For example, if I steal a chip from your plate without your permission, my maxim might be 'take other people's food without permission if you want it'.

This doesn't necessarily tell us whether the rules in our head, our maxims, are good rules or not. In order to decide this we need to rationally consider whether the rules we are following are categorical imperatives or merely hypothetical imperatives.

Hypothetical imperatives

A **hypothetical imperative** is a command that we would follow in order to achieve an end result. If your teacher gives the instruction 'do your homework', it may sound like an unconditional command, but it is not. It actually says 'do your homework (X) if you want to pass the course (Y)' or 'do your homework (X) if you wish to avoid detention (Y)'. It may be slightly odd, but there is nothing illogical in someone replying that they don't want to pass or that they don't mind detentions. Kant argues that if the command only applies in certain cases or is dependent on the outcome, then this is not a moral duty.

Categorical imperatives

A **categorical imperative** is a command which logically has to be followed. It does not depend upon the end results. Its logical form is simply 'Do X' or 'Don't do X'. Hence when you decide to act upon the rule 'Do not kill', it is not because you have an outcome in mind. There is something unconditional about the command. Kant offers three tests or formulations as to how we can decide whether a maxim is hypothetical or categorical: they are universal law, persons as ends and Kingdom of ends.

> **Key quote**
>
> All imperatives command either hypothetically or categorically ... if the action would be good simply as a means to something else, then the imperative would be hypothetical, but if the action is represented as good in itself, in accordance with reason, then the imperative is categorical.
>
> Kant, *Groundwork of the Metaphysics of Morals*

> **Key words**
>
> **Autonomy** Literally 'self-ruling', the belief that we are free and able to make our own decisions
>
> **Maxim** Another word for moral rules or principles. They are the things that we act upon
>
> **Hypothetical imperative** A moral obligation that is dependent upon desiring the goal in question
>
> **Categorical imperative** An unconditional moral obligation that we are able to work out using reason

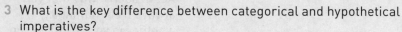

Now test yourself

3 What is the key difference between categorical and hypothetical imperatives?

4 Which imperative is more important for Kant and why?

3.4 Kant's three formulations

Kant suggests three ways that we can test whether our actions are categorical imperatives.

1 **Universal law.** Kant suggests that the action that we propose should be able to be made a universal law. We have to consider whether this is something that all people could logically do; if not, we shouldn't put ourselves above the law by being an exception.

   Example: Suppose I am planning to steal your work. If everyone were to steal things all the time this would be chaotic and illogical (if stealing is where you take things that are not yours and everyone was always stealing, then would anyone actually have anything that was theirs?). So stealing makes no sense – and I am not allowed to be the exception.

2 **Persons as ends.** Kant believes that human beings are rational and autonomous. This means that we have a duty to treat each other as persons (as 'ends' in themselves) and not as we would treat an object ('as a means to an end'). We can use objects but we ought not to use people.

   Example: Suppose your boyfriend breaks up with you but you want them back. You begin to date another boy in a bid to make your original boyfriend jealous. In doing so you are treating that boy as an object (a means to an end) and not as a person.

3 **Kingdom of ends.** In his final formulation, which in some ways might be seen as a combination of the other two, Kant asks us to imagine that we are part of the law-making council in a hypothetical perfect Kingdom of ends. If we were to live in this place where everyone always treated others as ends, would our maxim or proposed action be something that could be permitted?

   Example: Suppose someone hits you, it may be legally acceptable to hit them back. However, Kant's Kingdom of ends asks you to act based on how society ought to be rather than how it is. Hence it is difficult to see how hitting your assailant would be treating them as an end.

Kant's examples of categorical imperatives

It is worth noting that Kant himself gives us very few examples of possible imperatives that pass the tests above. Remember he thinks that we are rational and able to work these out for ourselves. His four main cases are:

1 That it is wrong to make a lying promise
2 That it is wrong to commit suicide
3 That it is wrong to neglect one's talent
4 That it is wrong to refrain from helping others.

Now test yourself

5 Give an example of an action that Kant thinks cannot be universalised.

Key words

Universal law The principle that we should only carry out those acts that we are able to will as a law for everyone at all times

Persons as ends The idea that human beings should be treated with dignity and respect, and not as mere objects

Kingdom of ends A hypothetical or imaginary state where people always act according to the moral rules and treat others as ends

Key quote

Act only according to the maxim by which you can at the same time will that it should become a universal law.

Kant, *Groundwork for the Metaphysics of Morals*

Key quote

Act in such a way that you always treat humanity, whether in your own person or in the person of any other, never simply as a means, but always at the same time as an end.

Kant, *Groundwork of the Metaphysics of Morals*

3.5 Applying Kantian ethics

There are a number of features of Kantian ethics that become apparent when it is applied to actual cases.

1 **Lying to murderers**. One of the more famous applications of Kantian ethics is the hypothetical case of a murderer asking if his next victim is hiding in a certain house. According to Kant's maxim of universalisation, we are morally required to tell the truth. Kant argues that we will have done our duty in doing so; it is the murderer not us that is behaving immorally.

Key point: Kant's ethics is **absolutist** in its approach; it allows no flexibility to the circumstances or the situation. Second, Kant is not concerned over the outcome; he argues that we cannot control the outcome. His ethics are completely **deontological**, focusing on the action itself.

2 **My sister's keeper**. In the film *My Sister's Keeper*, Anna is born by IVF in order to be a genetic match for her terminally ill sister, Kate. One of her kidneys is to be used for transplant as her sister's kidney is failing. This would be problematic for Kantian ethics as this involves using Anna, a person, as a means to an end.

Key point: Kantian ethics **values persons**. They are not just a commodity that can be used.

3 **Charity**. Much of our moral decision making is based on how we feel. As we watch TV or scroll through our news feed, we may on two different days see almost identical charity appeals. On one occasion we may give as we are moved by the suffering; yet on another day we may feel indifferent. For Kant this makes no sense; either it is our duty to help others where we can or it is not.

Key point: Kantian ethics is entirely **rational** and seeks to make decisions based on logic and not emotions. Our emotions are too inconsistent to give us clear moral duties.

4 **Business ethics**. A ruthless business owner may be able to make more money by paying employees the bare minimum and denying them regular breaks. He may also choose to overcharge customers when he can get away with it. Kant's ethics prevents this with his focus on treating persons with respect. In one of his own examples the shopkeeper should not just behave honestly because it is good for business. He should behave honestly because it is the right thing to do.

Key point: Kantian ethics with its respect for persons leads to the idea of rights and the dignity of human beings. Modern ideas of human rights owe much to Kant.

Now test yourself

6 What does Kant think we should do if confronted by a killer seeking the location of his next victim?

3.6 Assessing the idea of duty

The idea that ethical issues should be resolved entirely by the concept of duty raises a number of issues.

1 Duty is a useful concept as our inclinations and desires about what we want are subject to change. The concept of duty demands that we put our feelings aside in order to do the right thing.

2 A key issue, however, is the problem of conflicting duties. In our example of the murderer asking for the whereabouts of his next victim, we have a duty to tell the truth yet we also have a duty to save life. Kantian ethics does not give us a clear way of deciding which duty we should follow when duties conflict.

3 The concept of duty can also be abused. One way is when it becomes conflated with the idea of obedience to authority. The Nazis who were put on trial at Nuremberg argued that they were doing their duty. However, in response to this, a Kantian might point out that the problem is in the misunderstanding, not in the actual theory itself. No one who understands Kantian ethics and its respect for persons could allow the atrocities of the Nazi regime to take place.

Duty and God: The three postulates

A final issue with Kant's reliance on duty is the link to God. A key feature on Kantian ethics is doing duty for duty's sake regardless of any reward. Yet as we will see below, there is in fact a reward for duty.

For Kant there are three **postulates** – or assumptions – that have to be in place for morality to function.

1 **That we have free will**: If we are not genuinely free to do either the good thing or the evil thing then there can be no moral responsibility.

2 **That there is an afterlife, we are immortal**: Kant argues that morality requires the *summum bonum* (the highest good) to be achieved. This is where perfect virtue (good deeds) is rewarded by perfect happiness. This does not happen in this life but to say it ought to be achieved must mean that it can; so the *summum bonum* must occur in the next life.

3 **That God exists**: In order that the *summum bonum* actually occurs and goodness is rewarded by happiness, there must be a God who ensures the justice of the universe.

Kant does not think that these three things are proved; merely that they must be assumed practically in order for morality to exist.

> ### Key words
>
> **Postulates** Things that have to be assumed or are a basis for reasoning. For Kant, free will, immorality and God have to be postulated in order for morality to make sense
>
> *Summum bonum* The highest good, where virtue is rewarded by happiness

> ### Making links
>
> Kant's view on morality is that it is autonomous; it does not depend upon God. See the Developments in Christian Thought book, Chapter 5. One of the reasons he believes that God is not required is because like Rousseau, and unlike Augustine, he believes in the power of human nature to do good; humans are not damaged by original sin.

Now test yourself

7 How does the *summum bonum* link to God?

3.7 Discussing Kantian ethics

In addition to the discussion of duty, there are several other key strengths and weaknesses of Kantian ethics.

Strengths of Kantian ethics

1 The principle of universal law seems to provide a useful principle in making moral decisions. It bears some similarities to the golden rule of religion 'treat others as you would wish them to treat you'. It treats each person equally and stops us making ourselves a special case.
2 Following on from this, the appeal to concepts such as reason and duty make Kantian ethics impartial and less prone to personal bias.
3 Kantian ethics respects the intrinsic value of persons. This enables a concept of rights to be used. This is a favourable contrast with theories like utilitarianism where persons are only instrumentally valuable and the idea of rights is 'nonsense on stilts' (Bentham).

Weaknesses of Kantian ethics

1 Intuitively it seems that outcome does matter. Although we may have told the truth to the murderer seeking the whereabouts of his victim, we would feel guilty if our honesty led to their death. This suggests that Kant is wrong to ignore outcome.
2 Kantian ethics is too abstract and theoretical: it offers perfect solutions based on a hypothetical Kingdom of ends, yet it cannot cope with a real world where people may act in an immoral way and we have to respond. Likewise it doesn't fare too well in dilemmas where we are obliged to consider which is the lesser of two evils, for example, which of two dying people to save.
3 Kantian ethics is better at showing things we ought not to do rather than showing what we should do. There are a number of strange maxims that could be universalised and do not treat persons as a means to an end. There is no logical contradiction about 'standing on one leg every Wednesday', yet this is not really a moral duty.

Developing arguments on Kantian ethics

To access higher levels on the mark scheme points need to be discussed or developed rather than just stated. Below are some examples.

Proposed strength of Kantian ethics	Discussion/counter-argument
As with other absolutist theories, it offers clear and fixed guidelines. We are clear on how Kant's ethics apply.	However, this also presents a difficulty in that there is an inflexibility in Kant's thinking. While we may accept that stealing is generally wrong, an extreme situation where someone is starving may require a different response.
Kantian ethics is a secular theory. Unlike a theory such as Natural Law, there is no requirement to believe in God as the imperatives are worked out rationally rather than being given as commands by God.	Critics have suggested that Kant does not totally manage to escape the idea of God. His *summum bonum* is based on the idea that God exists to reward those who do their moral duty. In Kant's defence, he would argue this is the consequence of doing good rather than a motivation or means of making the decision.
Kantian ethics is rational and as such is not based on the changeable nature of our emotions, hence we get sound and well-reasoned moral decisions.	There are two potential issues with this. First, it makes an assumption about our capacity to reason. Thinkers such as Augustine and Barth might challenge this on the grounds of our fallen human nature. Second, some emotions such as compassion can be very powerful. It is strange to argue that an act of giving to charity is somehow more virtuous because the person in question did not feel like it.

3.8 Summary and exam tips

Exam checklist

● Explain how Kant uses the idea of duty in his ethical theory.
● Explain the difference between hypothetical and categorical imperatives.
● Explain the three formulations of the categorical imperative: universal law, end in itself, and the Kingdom of ends.
● Explain how Kant's ethics is based on assumptions about freedom, immortality and God.
● Assess whether Kantian ethics enables us to make good moral decisions.
● Consider whether the idea of doing your duty is what makes an action right or wrong.
● Consider criticisms of Kantian ethics, such as its rejection of emotions/love and its abstract and impractical nature.

Exam tip

When it comes to the practical application of Kant's ethics to topics such as business ethics or sexual ethics, the three formulations are the key aspects that can be applied. Ask yourself whether the action can be universalised, whether it treats persons as ends, and whether it would be permitted in a Kingdom of ends.

Typical mistake

Be careful with universal law. There is a tendency to over-simplify it to 'Would I like it if everyone did this?' More accurately, it is about whether the universalised action is logical or not. The paragraphs below illustrate the point.

Revision activity

There are a number of key words in Kantian ethics. Write these down on one set of cards and their definitions on another. Either on your own or with a friend, practise matching them up to help you learn the terms.

Sample answer

Basic explanation	Better explanation
Kant believes in the idea of universal law. This means that it would be wrong to do something if we would not like everyone to do this. Lying is wrong because if everyone were to lie then this would not be acceptable. Kant thinks that we should treat others as we wish to be treated.	Kant's first test for the categorical imperative is the idea of universal law. He argues that an action is only morally acceptable if we are able to universalise it; in other words we are able to 'will' that it become an action that could occur at all times and all places. For example, if we were to consider the action of lying then if everyone were to always tell lies, a logical contradiction would occur. Lying means saying something that is not true yet if everyone always did this then truth would no longer exist. Hence it would become impossible to define lying and the act of lying would be illogical.

Going further: John Rawls and the veil of ignorance

The political philosopher John Rawls (1921–2002) was influenced by Kantian ethics in his writings on justice. He argued that justice (or fairness) is whatever we would agree to from behind the veil of ignorance; this is a hypothetical idea where we would have to agree the moral and political laws we would wish to live by before knowing what our position in life would be. For example, we would ban racism and homophobia if we did not know whether we were to be born black or white, or gay or straight. Rawls also uses this logic, which owes much to Kant's universal law and treating persons with respect, to argue for redistribution of wealth; the very rich have a duty to help those whose misfortune it is to be born into poverty.

4 Utilitarianism

4.1 Introduction

The theory of **utilitarianism** argues that we should do whatever leads to the greatest good for the greatest number. Hence this theory is a teleological or consequentialist theory that decides the rightness or wrongness of an action based on the results produced. Utilitarianism (at least in its act version) does not follow moral rules. It is also a secular theory that regards the teaching of religion as irrelevant in moral decision making. This theory is associated with Jeremy Bentham (1748–1832) and John Stuart Mill (1806–1873), who are responsible for act and rule versions of utilitarianism, respectively.

> **Key word**
>
> **Utilitarianism** The ethical idea that we should always seek to achieve the greatest balance of good over evil

The specification says

Topic	Content	Key knowledge
Utilitarianism	• Utility	• The use of the significant concept of utility (seeking the greatest balance of good over evil, or pleasure over pain) in teleological and relativist approaches to ethics
	• The hedonic calculus	• What it is (calculating the benefit or harm of an act through its consequences) and its use as a measure of individual pleasure
	• Act utilitarianism	• What it is (calculating the consequences of each situation on its own merits) and its use in promoting the greatest amount of good over evil, or pleasure over pain
	• Rule utilitarianism	• What it is (following accepted laws that lead to the greatest overall balance of good over evil, or pleasure over pain) and its use in promoting the common good
Learners should have the opportunity to discuss issues raised by utilitarianism, including: • whether or not utilitarianism provides a helpful method of moral decision-making • whether or not an ethical judgement about something being good, bad, right or wrong can be based on the extent to which, in any given situation, utility is best served • whether or not it is possible to measure good or pleasure and then reach a moral decision.		

Now test yourself

1 What is the key idea involved in utilitarianism?
2 Utilitarianism is a teleological theory. What does this mean?

4.2 Bentham: utility and the hedonic calculus

The first great utilitarian thinker was Jeremy Bentham (1748–1832). Bentham was a legal and political thinker, as well as a moral philosopher. He was interested in both what was good for society and what was good for humans as individuals. Bentham's moral thinking starts with an observation about human nature.

Bentham on human nature

Bentham suggests that pain and pleasure are our masters. We instinctively seek pleasure and avoid pain. It seems that nature has built us this way. It is not God that has made us, nor are we driven by our logical reason. Our psychology is built on seeking pleasure and avoiding pain.

> **Key quote**
>
> Nature has placed mankind under the governance of two sovereign masters, pain and pleasure. It is for them alone to point out what we ought to do, as well as to determine what we shall do.
>
> Jeremy Bentham, *The Principles of Morals and Legislation* (1789)

Bentham on utility

Given that we are motivated by pleasure and pain, Bentham proposes one simple moral principle that both individuals and governments should adopt. The idea of **utility** (or usefulness) is that actions should be carried out if they produce more happiness, pleasure or goodness and are likely to prevent pain, misery and unhappiness. In *A Fragment on Government*, Bentham argues that 'it is the greatest happiness of the greatest number that is the measure of right and wrong'.

> **Key word**
>
> **Utility** The idea of 'usefulness' that we should do whatever is useful in increasing overall good and decreasing overall evil

> **Key quote**
>
> By the principle of utility is meant that principle which approves or disapproves of every action whatsoever. According to the tendency it appears to have to augment or diminish the happiness of the party whose interest is in question: or, what is the same thing in other words to promote or to oppose that happiness.
>
> Jeremy Bentham, *The Principles of Morals and Legislation* (1789)

Bentham rejects any appeal to the good of the country or the community. Communities are merely the sum of the individuals.

The hedonic calculus

In addition to suggesting that we are motivated by pleasure and pain and that the only moral principle needed is that we should do whatever is useful to achieve this end, Bentham also provides a method of calculating which course of action to take. This is known as the **hedonic calculus**.

He suggests that there are seven factors that should be taken into account when making a decision. In order to understand these, imagine that you have a sadistic teacher who offers to give you chocolate in class as long as you agree to be kicked in the shins each lesson.

> **Key word**
>
> **Hedonic calculus** A system for working out the amount of pleasure or pain involved in a course of action

Factor	What Bentham means	Example
Intensity	How strong is the pleasure or pain?	How much do you enjoy chocolate? How much does it hurt if you are kicked in the shin?
Duration	How long will the pleasure or pain last?	How long does the taste of chocolate last? When will the pain subside in your shin?
Certainty	How likely is it that the pleasure or pain will actually occur?	Are you sure you like that particular type of chocolate? Are you sure they will kick you hard?
Propinquity	How soon will the pleasure or pain occur?	Would it change things if the chocolate or the kick in the shins was delivered at a much later date?
Fecundity	How likely is it that the pleasure will lead to further pleasures?	Will more chocolate follow?
Purity	How likely is it that pain will come from the original pleasure?	For example, will the pleasure of stolen chocolate lead to the pain of being arrested?
Extent	How many people will be affected?	What if 100 people get chocolate if 10 are kicked in the shin?

Bentham argues that when faced with a moral decision you should weigh up all the possible pleasures and pains using the criteria above and work out whether overall there would be more pleasure or pain.

Now test yourself

TESTED ☐

3 What is the utility principle?
4 What are the seven factors Bentham considers in his hedonic calculus?

Typical mistake

Be careful when explaining utilitarianism. Sometimes students oversimplify utilitarianism by suggesting that if five people want X but one person wants Y, then X should be done. Utilitarianism is not just a matter of counting votes. If the one person is in severe agony to give five people slight pleasure, then this would not be permitted by Bentham.

4.3 Mill's utilitarianism

REVISED ☐

John Stuart Mill (1806–1873) is the second of the great classical utilitarians. Mill is keen to keep the central idea of utilitarianism but is aware of some issues that affect Bentham's version.

Possible weaknesses in Bentham's version

- The focus on pleasure is too narrow – there's more to life than food, sex and parties.
- It leads to appalling consequences – theoretically Bentham's version could justify gang rape.
- The hedonic calculus can be too complex if it has to be applied in each situation – not quick to get decisions.

Higher and lower pleasures

Mill supports the utility principle, but rejects Bentham's hedonic calculus. For Mill, quality of pleasure is more important than quantity. There are certain pleasures that are higher pleasures and other pleasures that are merely lower pleasures.

Key quote

A being of higher faculties requires more to make him happy … It is better to be a human being dissatisfied than a pig satisfied; better to be Socrates dissatisfied than a fool satisfied.

J.S. Mill, *Utilitarianism*, 1863

A pig is an easy creature to satisfy. It does not mind the quality of its food and is happy to roll in mud. As humans, we are capable of greater pleasures so even if our lives are not the best, they are still to be preferred over the life of the pig. Likewise the deep thinking philosopher, even if unhappy, is in a better place than a shallow fool.

For Mill, the higher pleasures are intellectual and social, those things that as human beings we are able to experience. The lower pleasures – food, sex and sleep – are pleasures but are not as important. Mill argues that all 'competent judges' when given a choice between the two would prefer the higher pleasures.

When Mill refers to higher pleasures, he is referring to happiness in a broader sense than Bentham. Mill is to some extent thinking of *Eudaimonia* – the idea of happiness and human flourishing.

Key word

Eudaimonia Flourishing and living well, the ultimate end that all actions should lead towards

Making links

Linked to Mill's view of utilitarianism is his political and ethical non-harm principle. He argues that the only reason a government should impose laws is to prevent people from harming others. Other than this, we should be free to pursue our own course in life. It is this principle that leads Mill to argue for the legalisation of gay sex (see Chapter 9, Sexual ethics).

Now test yourself

TESTED

5 Imagine you are J.S. Mill. Sort the list below into higher and lower pleasures: eating cake, reading a newspaper, organising a community event, attending a philosophy class, drinking beer, attending a concert, chatting with a friend, sleeping.

4.4 Act and rule utilitarianism

REVISED

Act utilitarians believe that decisions should be made on each individual situation or action. Rule utilitarians consider issues generally and make rules that cover a range of situations.

Act utilitarianism

Act utilitarianism aims to produce a balance of good over evil in each case. It takes situations on a case-by-case basis. Bentham's hedonic calculus approach is an example of this. Hence act utilitarianism may give different answers to an issue because of the different contexts. There may be a greater good or happiness brought about by stealing a loaf of bread to feed a starving family, but the same shoplifter would be wrong to steal makeup for a wealthy individual.

The case-by-case decision making of act utilitarianism is both a strength and a weakness of the theory. It allows flexibility to the situation but takes considerable time to weigh up all the complex factors in each situation.

Rule utilitarianism

Rule utilitarianism also aims at the greatest balance of good over evil, but has the common good of society rather than individuals as its starting point. A key difference of Mill's utilitarianism over that of Bentham is that Mill can be seen as a rule utilitarian. It is still utilitarianism as the reason we are adopting rules is that our experience has shown us that

Key words

Act utilitarianism The idea that we should always perform the act that leads to the greatest balance of good over evil

Rule utilitarianism The idea that we should always follow the rule that generally leads to the greatest balance of good over evil

these actions tend to lead to the common good; our experience of stealing would lead us to say that this typically does not lead to a greater good and hence is wrong. This is illustrated by Ahluwalia and Bowie in the example of the Highway Code. Whilst it may suit me to drive differently and it may not matter in a specific instance, there are fewer accidents overall if we all adhere to the rules.

Mill's own example comes from his principles of non-harm and liberty. In allowing freedom for individuals to live as they wish, we are allowing individuals to experiment with different ways of living. This may lead to discoveries of better approaches to life and better rules. We may discover that homosexuality is not harmful and hence change our rules accordingly. This freedom for all may mean that some waste their lives experimenting with drink or drugs, but overall allowing humans freedom is beneficial.

An advantage of this view is that it is quicker in terms of decision making to apply a rule than to attempt to weigh up all the factors involved in each case. However, the disadvantage comes in cases where rules clash. We may have rules about telling the truth and about saving life but if we are asked by a murderer where their next victim is hiding we cannot satisfy both rules.

> **Typical mistake**
>
> Rule utilitarianism is difficult to understand and may seem a contradiction in terms. It is utilitarian in that the rules adopted are those which lead to the greater good. They are not like the rules that religion may prescribe which are timeless and fixed. Rule utilitarians recognise that the rules can be changed if required by the greater good.

Now test yourself

TESTED

6 What is the main difference between act and rule utilitarianism?

4.5 Applying utilitarianism

REVISED

There are a number of key features of utilitarianism that become apparent when the theory is applied to practical issues or hypothetical scenarios.

1 **Trolley problems**. Trolley problems are hypothetical cases devised by Philippa Foot to test our moral thinking. If a train is heading towards a group of children and you are able to divert it so that it runs over one elderly tramp, then you should do so according to utilitarianism even if you are responsible for his death.
   Key point: Utilitarianism is entirely concerned with the outcome. It is a **teleological** theory. The action itself is not judged and is thus less important.

2 **The dying billionaire**. Louis Pojman gives a hypothetical case of a billionaire who on his death bed makes you promise to give all his money to his favourite sports team so that they can win the league. However, you see an advertisement that suggests that a similar amount of money could prevent 100,000 people dying of starvation. It seems obvious that you should break your promise and give the money to charity.
   Key point: Utilitarianism is demanding. It requires that you set aside your personal happiness in getting the latest CD of your favourite band. That money could save an entire village!

3 **Executing the innocent**. Suppose a murder is committed in a town where there is racial tension. The crime is believed to be racially motivated. The sheriff knows that the real perpetrator is dead, but cannot prove it. If he were to arrest and frame a passing tramp, tensions in the community would be eased and no one need ever know.
   Key point: Utilitarians do not put much weight on concepts such as justice and rights unless the outcome requires it.

4 **On sexuality**. Both Bentham and Mill were keen social reformers who argued for the decriminalisation of homosexuality, as well as

> **Typical mistake**
>
> Be careful not to assume that utilitarianism is selfish and focuses on our own pleasure. If anything it is the opposite and makes great demands of us. Utilitarianism requires that we sacrifice our own happiness if it leads to the happiness of others.

> **Key quote**
>
> The power of sacrificing their own greatest good for the good of others ... the only self-renunciation which it applauds is devotion to the happiness ... of others; either of mankind collectively, or of individuals.
>
> J.S. Mill, *Utilitarianism*, 1863

equal rights for women. Both were out of step with the thinking of their day. Yet on both issues, it was possible to argue that greater good could be achieved by challenging existing thinking.

Key point: Utilitarianism is **progressive** and modern in its approach.

5 **On euthanasia**. Utilitarianism tends to support the right of individuals to end their lives by euthanasia if they wish. This has particularly been argued by modern utilitarian Peter Singer, who argues that the greatest good is found in satisfying people's preferences (known as preference utilitarianism). This challenges the notion of sanctity of life by looking at factors that may improve or limit the overall quality of life.

Key point: Utilitarianism favours quality of life over sanctity of life.

6 **On business ethics**. A utilitarian approach to business can be shown in the work of the famous economist Adam Smith (1723–1790). He argued that fairness in business was economic good sense. If we treat customers and workers well, we are likely to make more money in the long run than if we cheat or exploit others.

Key point: Utilitarianism has an instrumental approach to actions. Things are not good in themselves but only in regard to how they help the greater good to be achieved.

4.6 Assessing utilitarianism

REVISED

Key strengths of utilitarianism

- **Impartiality**. Utilitarianism requires that we are objective and that we do not resolve ethical dilemmas by having favourites or resorting to personal biases.
- **Secular**. Utilitarianism, unlike a number of other moral theories, does not resort to religion to justify how we should act. This makes utilitarianism an attractive theory for a more secular age.
- **Maximising happiness is a good aim**. It would be strange to argue that we should not value happiness or that we should set out to do things that cause more overall unhappiness.
- **It is a straightforward theory**. Utilitarianism is not difficult to understand or apply. It offers a decision procedure that enables moral dilemmas to be solved.
- **It is progressive**. Utilitarianism has been a progressive morality that has enabled out of date ideas, such as the banning of homosexual acts or the oppression of women, to be challenged. Utilitarian thinkers have been at the forefront of these changes. Modern utilitarians, such as Singer, continue to stand up for the poor and campaign for animal rights.
- **It is democratic**. Everyone's happiness is taken into account and each person counts as one in decision making. There are no favourites or special exemptions. In theory, presidents and paupers are treated alike.

Exam tip

These points are stated unchallenged as strengths of utilitarianism. To score high marks, there needs to be discussion as to the relative strength of each point. For instance, we stated that utilitarianism is straightforward to apply. You may wish to present a counterargument as to why this may not be the case by explaining all the different factors in the hedonic calculus in any given decision. An example of the sort of reflection of points that might be needed is given below.

4.7 Criticisms of utilitarianism

REVISED

There are a number of possible criticisms of utilitarianism, particularly of Bentham's version.

- It is not clear how we are to measure pleasure and pain. If I enjoy kicking people but you do not enjoy being kicked, whose pleasure or pain is greater? Things that are measurable have clear units, e.g. metres, volts or joules. How can pleasure and pain be measured?
- Utilitarianism requires prediction of the future. In order to establish what the greater good will be, we have to predict future consequences. Yet the future is not always clear. The baby we save may turn out to be a cruel dictator.
- Although in theory each person is regarded equally by utilitarianism, there is potentially a problem for minority groups. For example, if a majority of a society held homophobic views, what would prevent them from imposing their belief that homosexuality was harmful? To some extent, Mill is aware of this criticism and warns against the 'tyranny of the majority'.
- The swine ethic problem: Bentham's utilitarianism was called a swine ethic because it seemed to permit such horrors as gang rape (at least in theory). Although this was not intended by Bentham, and may be answered by later versions of the theory, the worry remains that there are no absolute boundaries in utilitarianism and horrors such as the torture of children may be permitted in extreme situations.
- Pleasure and happiness are not the only goods. Utilitarianism assumes that pleasure or happiness are the ultimate good. There are other views of what goodness is. Obedience to God's commands is the ultimate good in some world views; the development of good character traits is the ultimate aim in the theory of virtue ethics.
- Pleasure and pain may be dependent on the individual. We may have different views on what leads to happiness. This may make Singer's version, based on satisfying preferences, a more viable option than classical utilitarianism.

Now test yourself

TESTED

7 Imagine you are exploring an underground cave with eight friends. As the water begins to rise you make your way to the only remaining exit. One of your number, 'Big Jake', goes first but gets stuck. The rising water threatens to drown you all and push Jake out. However, you have a stick of dynamite which you could attach to Jake, blowing him up and making the exit wider. What would a utilitarian suggest?
8 What are the main strengths of utilitarianism?

Exam tip

One possible strategy when assessing utilitarianism is to recognise that there are different types of utilitarianism. You might argue that not all types of utilitarianism are guilty of each of the weaknesses. Bentham's utilitarianism has attracted many criticisms, but are Mill and Singer equally guilty? Can they deal with some of the objections?

Going further: Developing arguments on utilitarianism

Criticism of utilitarianism	Counter-argument or response
Utilitarianism is too demanding: the theory demands that we care for everyone equally and do not prioritise our own family when rescuing people from burning buildings. It also gives us no rest. We should not have an evening in front of the TV or with friends while there are still people dying of starvation in the world. There is never a good enough reason to go to the cinema while there are homeless people who would benefit far more from your £10.	One way to counter this might be to suggest that a rule about overall happiness might involve a balanced life. If everyone were constantly giving and becoming exhausted in the process, then the overall happiness would be decreased.
The problem of moral agency: Bernard Williams gives the famous example of 'Jim and the Indians'. He asks you to imagine that you arrive in a town to find ten innocent political prisoners about to be shot. The corrupt captain of the guard suggests he will release all of them if you take the honour of shooting one yourself. A utilitarian should find this an easy decision to make; it is saving nine lives by taking one. Yet Williams notes that there is a problem. Utilitarianism ignores the problem of 'moral agency'. Are we really able to do this and live with ourselves afterwards? Utilitarianism ignores our integrity.	One response might be that we really do have to be brave and carry out the act that is the lesser of two evils. After all, we are responsible not just for our actions but also our omissions – if we could have saved lives but we did not. If we value our integrity over the lives and happiness of others then it is difficult to argue that we are doing the right thing.
Utilitarians do not value justice: the example of the sheriff who frames the innocent tramp in order to prevent unrest (above) shows that utilitarians do not value justice or human rights. Bentham himself once suggested that talk of human rights was 'nonsense on stilts'.	One response to this might be to argue that 'rights' may have a value; it makes society better to assume rights. But this is unconvincing as utilitarians will ditch these rights if the situation requires, arguing that more innocent people are likely to be harmed by our inaction.

Now test yourself

TESTED

9 What are the key weaknesses of utilitarianism?

> **Exam checklist**
> - Explain the ideas of utility and the hedonic calculus.
> - Explain the theory of act utilitarianism.
> - Explain the theory of rule utilitarianism.
> - Assess whether utilitarianism enables us to make good moral decisions.
> - Consider the extent to which utility is the thing to consider in moral decision making.
> - Consider issues with utilitarianism, including whether it is possible to measure pleasure and pain.

Sample work

In order to do well in the exam, you will need to develop and discuss points rather than just stating them. Have a look at the difference in the paragraph below.

Basic paragraph	Better paragraph
Utilitarianism is a good theory as it treats everyone equally. It does not matter about your race or gender. Utilitarianism can be seen as a weak theory as it does not help minorities.	First, it is claimed that utilitarianism supports equality. Each person counts for one and their happiness is equally valuable regardless of their gender, race or sexuality. However, the initial impression is again misleading. While my happiness may be counted, if for whatever reason I find myself in a minority then my happiness will ultimately be discounted in the end in order for the greater good to be achieved. If hypothetically Hitler could have shown that the removal of the Jews would indeed lead to the greater good then this minority would in no way be protected. Hence it is difficult to say that this point is a clear and obvious strength.

Going further: Singer and preference utilitarianism

One popular modern version of utilitarianism is preference utilitarianism as held by Peter Singer (1946–) and others. It attempts to address one of the key issues with the classical utilitarianism of Bentham and Mill, which is the assumption that we all have a similar view of goodness or happiness.

Preference utilitarianism argues that people should be allowed to pursue their preferences as long as it does not interfere with anyone else's pursuit of happiness. The morally good thing to do is that which maximises the satisfaction of the preferences of most people. Hence a preference approach focuses more on minimising suffering and harm rather than increasing pleasure. In his text *The Life You Can Save*, he argues that we have a responsibility in the western world to give generously to developing countries; in doing so we can minimise pointless deaths and allow others greater opportunity to achieve their goals. Singer requires that we adopt the perspective of the impartial observer in order to weigh up the greatest balance of good.

5 Euthanasia

5.1 Introduction

In February 1993 almost four years after being fatally injured in the 1989 Hillsborough disaster Tony Bland died. In the intervening four years he had been kept alive by machines in a state where, according to Lord Justice Hoffmann, 'his body is alive, but he has no life in the sense that even the most handicapped but conscious human being has a life' (quoted in Singer, *Rethinking Life and Death*). In a landmark court ruling it was agreed that the feeding tubes keeping Tony Bland alive could be withdrawn. The topic of euthanasia, of which the above case may be an example, raises a number of key issues: it appears to put the concepts of sanctity of life and quality of life into direct opposition; it raises issues around autonomy, specifically whether there is such a thing as the 'right to die'; and it requires careful distinction between various actions or omissions which may (or may not) be regarded as euthanasia. In addition to the above, in studying this topic, the ethical theories of Natural Law and situation ethics will be applied to this topic.

> **Key word**
>
> **Assisted suicide** A person who wishes to die is helped to die by another person. They may or may not have a serious or terminal illness

The specification says

Topic	Content	Key knowledge
Euthanasia	Key ideas, including: ● sanctity of life	The religious origins of this concept (that human life is made in God's image and is therefore sacred in value)
	● quality of life	The secular origins of this significant concept (that human life has to possess certain attributes in order to have value)
	● voluntary euthanasia	What it is (that a person's life is ended at their request or with their consent) and its use in the case of incurable or terminal illness
	● non-voluntary euthanasia	What it is (that a person's life is ended without their consent but with the consent of someone representing their interests) and its use in the case of a patient who is in a persistent vegetative state
	Learners should have the opportunity to discuss issues raised by euthanasia, including: ● the application of Natural Law and situation ethics to euthanasia ● whether or not the religious concept of sanctity of life has any meaning in twenty-first century medical ethics ● whether or not a person should or can have complete autonomy over their own life and decisions made about it ● whether or not there is a moral difference between medical intervention to end a patient's life and medical non-intervention to end a patient's life.	

Now test yourself

1 What does euthanasia mean?
2 What is the difference between active and passive euthanasia?

5.2 Sanctity of life and quality of life

The law and key words

At a simple level, **euthanasia**, although legal in some countries such as Holland and Switzerland, is illegal in the UK.

- **Suicide** has been decriminalised, but it is still an offence to assist someone in committing suicide.
- It is legally wrong to administer **active euthanasia** – to do something that directly causes death.
- The Tony Bland case provided a precedent whereby, in certain extreme circumstances, **non-voluntary euthanasia** is in effect permitted. This is also an example of **passive euthanasia**, which involves the withdrawal of treatment that is keeping a patient alive. This indirectly causes death.

The sanctity of life

The **sanctity of life** is a key aspect of religious ethics. In Christian ethics, it refers to the idea that life is special and valuable because it is God-given. Despite the belief that humans are fallen and damaged by sin, each person is still created in the 'image of God'. This means that it is morally wrong to take life. Each life has intrinsic value regardless of its quality or usefulness to us. The following references from the Bible are often used to support the idea of the sanctity of life.

- 'So God created humankind in his own image, in the image of God he created them' (*Genesis* 1:27). This image of God is understood in various ways such as the capacity for rationality, the divine spark within humans, or the ability to make moral decisions.
- 'You shall not murder' (*Exodus* 20:13). The command against taking a life is one of the Ten Commandments. Although it is possible to debate whether the commandment is about murder specifically or killing more generally, the principle of the importance of respecting life is upheld.
- 'The Lord gave, and the Lord has taken away; blessed be the name of the Lord' (*Job* 1:21). It is for God to decide the moment of birth and the moment of death; it cannot be a human decision as our lives are not our own but God's.

The quality of life

The **quality of life** principle takes the view that whether life is valuable depends on whether it is worth living. Some thinkers base the decision on whether quality of life exists around possession of life's goods such as happiness and freedom from pain. Others argue that quality of life can be found in possession of autonomy (see section 5.3, Autonomy and euthanasia). The utilitarian philosopher Peter Singer takes such a view and argues for replacing the traditional sanctity of life ethics with five quality of life commandments:

1 Recognise that the worth of human life varies.
2 Take responsibility for the consequences of your decisions (to save or end life).
3 Respect a person's desire to live or die.
4 Bring children into the world only if they are wanted.
5 Do not discriminate on the basis of species.

Key words

Euthanasia Literally 'a good death' (from the Greek *Eu* meaning well or good and *Thanatos* meaning death)

Suicide A person makes a voluntary choice and takes their own life

Active euthanasia A treatment is given that directly causes the death of the individual

Non-voluntary euthanasia Where a severely or terminally ill person's life is ended without their consent, perhaps because they are unable to give consent

Passive euthanasia A treatment is withheld and this indirectly causes the death of the individual

Key words

Sanctity of life The idea that life is intrinsically sacred or valuable

Quality of life The idea that life's value depends on certain attributes or goods, for example, happiness, autonomy

OCR A Level Religious Studies: Religion and Ethics   35

Summary

The key differences between sanctity of life and quality of life can be seen in the table below.

Sanctity of life	Quality of life
Religious view	Secular view
Intrinsic value of life	Instrumental view
Supported by Natural Law	Supported by situation ethics and utilitarianism
Absolute	Conditional

5.3 Autonomy and euthanasia

REVISED

Linked to quality of life, and in direct opposition to the sanctity of life, is the principle of **autonomy**. This principle states that humans should be free to make decisions about their own future. It is a key feature of utilitarian thinking and can be traced back to J.S. Mill's non-harm principle: whilst the government or other authority may restrict our freedom if we are about to harm someone else, they have no right to restrict our freedom with regard to ourselves. If we wish to harm ourselves we should be permitted to do so. Likewise Singer's preference utilitarianism argues that humans should be free to pursue their own desires and interests where possible. This autonomy includes the right to make our own decisions about our death.

Autonomy and euthanasia

Supporters of euthanasia appeal to the idea of autonomy. It seems to be a key aspect in determining our own lives that we have the ability to determine the time and manner of our own death. In the case of **voluntary euthanasia**, this may appear fairly straightforward; however, the leading British philosopher Jonathan Glover has suggested several checks on whether someone should be assisted to die.

This implies some external judgement as to the patient's quality of life as well as their mental state. If they are making the decision in a diminished mental state then they are not truly autonomous.

The issue of autonomy is more complicated in cases of non-voluntary euthanasia, particularly where a patient, perhaps like Tony Bland, is in a persistent vegetative state (PVS). If the patient has given instructions about what their wishes would be if they were in such a case, then arguably their autonomy is being respected. Where there are no explicit instructions, opponents of euthanasia worry that ending life may not only disregard the principle of the sanctity of life, but may also lead to a slippery slope where euthanasia is practised more widely.

> **Key words**
>
> **Autonomy** Literally 'self-ruling', the belief that we are free and able to make own decisions
>
> **Voluntary euthanasia** Where a person's life is ended at their own request. Usually this is done by another individual and is because of a terminal illness

> **Key quote**
>
> I must be convinced that your decision is a serious one; it must be properly thought out, not merely the result of a temporary emotional state. I must also think your decision is a reasonable one.
>
> Glover, *Causing Death and Saving Lives*

Now test yourself

TESTED

3 What is meant by non-voluntary euthanasia?
4 What Biblical passages might a Christian use to defend the idea of sanctity of life?

5.4 Acts and omissions

Is there a distinction between medical intervention to end life and medical non-intervention to end a life?

The Hippocratic Oath

The Greek physician Hippocrates (460–370 BE) states that it would be wrong for a doctor to do something that would cause the death of a person. However, in other writings, he suggests that it is pointless to continue to treat those who are overcome by a disease and for whom medicine is powerless. It is this distinction that provides the background for the modern discussion of acts and omissions. Roughly speaking, an 'act' which causes death is morally (and legally) wrong but an omission (stopping a treatment where the treatment is prolonging the inevitable death and increasing the suffering of the patient) may not be morally wrong.

> **Key quote**
>
> I will neither give a deadly drug to anybody if asked for it, nor will I make a suggestion to that effect.
>
> Part of the Hippocratic Oath taken by doctors

Rachels' challenging acts and omissions

The American philosopher James Rachels (1941–2003) has offered a thought experiment to suggest that the distinction between actively killing and passively letting someone die may not be helpful.

- Suppose Smith will inherit a fortune if his young nephew dies. One evening he drowns his nephew in the bath and arranges the scene to look like an accident. The nephew's death is an 'act' of Smith.
- Suppose Jones will also inherit a fortune if his young nephew dies. As he enters the bathroom, he sees his nephew slip and hit his head and slowly drown. He watches and does nothing to save the nephew. The nephew's death is an 'omission'; Jones could have saved him.

The traditional idea of acts and omissions says that Smith is guiltier than Jones. He certainly would be legally, but is he actually worse morally? Rachels argues that both cases are equally bad and when we consider the issue of euthanasia, passive euthanasia by omission may even be crueller as death may take longer.

Glover on ordinary and extraordinary means

Jonathan Glover suggests that the distinction between acts and omissions may not be so clear cut. This is because our actions and our omissions may involve ordinary and extraordinary means depending on whether the proposed treatment is something ordinary such as food and water or whether it involves highly expensive medical technology which would be an extraordinary means.

Glover suggests there are at least five options with regard to euthanasia.
1 Take all possible steps to preserve life.
2 Take all ordinary steps to preserve life but not use extraordinary means.
3 Not killing but taking no steps to preserve life.
4 An act which, while not intending to kill, has death as a possible foreseen consequence.
5 The deliberate act of killing.

However, we may debate what is or is not extraordinary means.

Peter Singer also questions the distinction between acts and omissions. Using the Tony Bland case, he asks us to consider whether the removal of the feeding tube was an 'act' that led to his death, or an 'omission', i.e. they were now omitting to feed him.

5.5 Natural Law and euthanasia

Natural Law opposes euthanasia for a number of reasons. However, in doing so it is important to distinguish between allowing someone to die naturally, which the theory may support, and cutting life short, which is always morally wrong.

Applying Natural Law

The key precept of Natural Law argues for the preservation of life. Life is intrinsically valuable and should not be shortened. Natural Law is dependent on the Divine Law revealed by God. Key texts such as the Ten Commandments and *Job* 1:21 'God gives and God takes away' seem to count against euthanasia. Following on from this, it would be difficult for someone to claim they were worshipping God, one of the five primary precepts, if they were shortening someone's life.

It could also be argued that the practice of euthanasia would undermine the stability of society; a society where life was not valued could not be an ordered society. People may fear hospital treatment. To end life by euthanasia instead of preserving life is an apparent good as opposed to a real good.

However, the principle of double effect may allow pain relief, such as morphine, even though administering such a drug may shorten life. This is acceptable provided the intention is to relieve pain and the shortening of life is an unintended secondary effect. Natural Law also draws a distinction between ordinary (natural) and extraordinary means. Thus a sick person is obliged to take treatment by ordinary means, such as food and water, but an extraordinary treatment which is risky and may not work could be refused.

> **Key quote**
>
> Discontinuing medical procedures that are burdensome, dangerous, extraordinary, or disproportionate to the expected outcome can be legitimate.
>
> *Catechism of the Catholic Church*, 2278–2279

> **Typical mistake**
>
> Students often wrongly assume that applying an ethical theory to an issue, as above, is AO2 but it is in fact AO1 (knowledge and understanding). AO2 is evaluation (asking how good a response the ethical theory provides).

Assessing Natural Law

It can be argued that Natural Law gives a good answer on euthanasia because ...	It can be argued that Natural Law does not give a good answer on euthanasia because ...
• It upholds the intrinsic value of life	• Its religious foundations make it seem outdated
• The principle of double effect gives a sensible flexibility to relieve pain when there is no prospect of saving the life	• It is legalistic and shows no compassion to the pain and suffering experienced by many terminally ill people
• It prevents humans from abusing power over others and putting themselves in the place of God	• The focus on sanctity of life means that the concepts of quality of life and individual autonomy are not seen as important

Now test yourself

5 What is the difference between ordinary and extraordinary means? Use an example to illustrate each of these ideas.
6 How does the Hippocratic Oath affect the attitude of medical professionals to the topic of euthanasia?

5.6 Situation ethics and euthanasia

Joseph Fletcher (1905–1991), the founder of situation ethics, served as president of 'Euthanasia Society of America' and his own example below of a patient declining life-sustaining treatment seems to support euthanasia.

Case study

Suppose the terminally ill man referenced in Chapter 2 were to refuse treatment and thus shorten his own life, or even speed up his own death through an act of euthanasia, this would not necessarily be wrong. Although Fletcher does not explicitly suggest he should refuse treatment, the implication given is that this could be the most loving outcome.

Applying situation ethics

- Situation ethics has 'personalism' as one of its key principles. It is people and their welfare rather than the keeping of laws that is at the heart of ethics.
- Situation ethics considers the quality of life as more significant than the sanctity of life.
- Situation ethics rejects legalism in favour of asking what is the most loving thing to do. Rules such as 'do not kill' are *sophia* (general rules of wisdom) according to Fletcher, but can be broken when love demands it.
- The theory is relativist in its approach. Fletcher states that 'love's decisions are made situationally, not prescriptively'. In his 1954 book, *Morals and Medicine*, he argues that the patient's medical condition has to be the starting point for any decisions in medical ethics. This is not a total endorsement of euthanasia, but a recognition that there are cases where this is the right option.

> **Key quote**
>
> It is whether we can justify taking it into our own hands, as human beings, to hasten death for ourselves (suicide) or for others (mercy killing) out of compassion. The answer in my view is clearly yes.
>
> Fletcher, *Essays in Biomedical Ethics*

> **Exam tip**
>
> When considering whether an ethical theory has a good approach to an ethical issue, look at the general strengths and weaknesses of the ethical theory and consider whether these apply to the issue that you are considering.

Assessing situation ethics

It can be argued that situation ethics is a good approach to euthanasia because …	It can be argued that situation ethics is not a good approach to euthanasia because …
It is flexible to individual situations, it recognises that no two situations regarding euthanasia are the same	Potentially 'do the most loving thing' is vague; what the most loving thing is may be subjective – a matter of opinion or perspective
Agape love, if correctly understood, is about ensuring the best possible outcome for the persons involved	Situation ethics has a number of the weaknesses of utilitarianism in that it requires a prediction of the future: what the most loving outcome is may not be absolutely certain

Now test yourself

7 Which of the primary precepts can be used when discussing Natural Law's approach to euthanasia?

8 Does situation ethics favour sanctity of life or quality of life? Explain your answer.

5.7 Assessing the relevance of sanctity of life

The case for sanctity of life

- There are concerns that if we do not uphold the supreme value of life this may lead to poorer treatment of patients or people feeling they are a burden on resources.
- The idea that life is special in all forms is not a bad idea. Modern ideas of rights have their origins in this idea and attempt to express a similar sentiment.
- Natural Law upholds the intrinsic value of life. Preservation of innocent life is one of its five primary precepts
- In the Bible, it states that 'The Lord gave and the Lord has taken away' (*Job* 1:21). In making decisions about life-ending treatments we may be guilty of presuming to know more than God.

The case against sanctity of life

- The sanctity of life assumes a religious worldview which many people in the twenty-first century no longer share.
- Sanctity of life says that life must be saved at all costs whether there is a good chance of treatment working or whether it is almost impossible. Yet technology and medical knowledge has advanced greatly and we are now able to know which lives can and cannot be saved; we no longer need to value life at all costs.
- Situation ethics rejects overly legalistic interpretations of the sanctity of life. It is far more important to work on a case-by-case basis attempting to do the most loving thing for the people involved.
- The suffering of patients may be unnecessarily increased if we preserve life at all costs.
- Peter Singer argues that sanctity of life is part of an old-fashioned traditional ethic that needs to be replaced. It directly goes against autonomy and control. Singer argues that people ought to have the freedom to make decisions about their lives for themselves.

Developing arguments on sanctity of life

The slippery slope argument

Opponents of euthanasia worry that changes to the law on euthanasia may be the beginning of a slippery slope where respect for life is reduced and pressure may be exerted on those who are vulnerable, such as the elderly or disabled. They may agree to euthanasia because they wrongly feel they are a burden to society. Opponents of euthanasia see a precedent for their slippery slope argument in the issue of abortion. When abortion was legalised, it was envisaged that it may be a few thousand cases per year for medical reasons. Currently, there are over 180,000 abortions in the UK each year.

Peter Singer has responded to the slippery slope argument for euthanasia. He cites a review conducted in the Netherlands where euthanasia is legal. There were around 48,000 end-of-life decisions in the time period studied; there were only two cases where it was possible that patients' lives had been ended against their will, although equally the two cases could also be explained by poor documentation.

> **Exam tip**
>
> Note that the wording in the specification refers to the relevance of the idea of the sanctity of life in the twenty-first century. This is a slightly more subtle question than whether sanctity of life is true or not.

Now test yourself

9 What is the slippery slope argument? How might it apply to euthanasia?

5.8 Summary and exam tips

Exam checklist
- Explain in detail the ideas of sanctity of life and quality of life.
- Explain what is meant by voluntary and non-voluntary euthanasia.
- Explain and assess how well the theory of Natural Law addresses euthanasia.
- Explain and assess how well the theory of situation ethics addresses euthanasia.
- Consider whether the sanctity of life is important in twenty-first century ethics.
- Assess whether a person should have complete control and autonomy over their own life and death.
- Consider the moral significance of acting to end a life or omitting to act to save a life.

Sample work

Assess the view that situation ethics is of no help with regard to the issue of euthanasia. (40 marks)

Looking carefully at the question above a candidate may work out the following:
- The command word 'Assess' steers the focus. It is important that the essay is an argument not just an explanation of issues in euthanasia or what situation ethics says.
- The focus needs to be on situation ethics. While another ethical theory, such as Natural Law, could be used as a contrast to bring out strengths or weaknesses of situation ethics, it must not distract from what the question is asking.
- 'The issue of euthanasia' is broad and allows a focus on different types of euthanasia. It may be worth distinguishing different ideas.
- 'Of no help' is quite a sweeping statement. It may be worth focusing on the 'no', which implies a complete uselessness of situation ethics in this case. Your conclusion could agree with this, disagree or offer something in between – that situation ethics is of some help.

Typical mistake

It is very easy to glance at exam questions such as the one above, pick out a key word such as euthanasia, and write pretty much all you know about the topic. The key to writing a good Religious Studies essay is selection of material. This involves making decisions about the material you have learned: what goes in and what stays out.

Sample conclusion

The conclusion and comment below illustrate the danger of missing the point of a question

Basic conclusion	Comment
In conclusion, it can be seen that situation ethics has a rule that it always supports euthanasia. This is because ending someone's life by an injection is always the most loving thing to do.	The candidate has missed the point of the question. 'Assess' requires that you make a judgement about how good the theory is, not that you just explain what the theory says. The idea that there is a 'rule' suggests the candidate doesn't really get situation ethics. Also there are different types of euthanasia, not just active.

Going further: Personhood

Linked to the idea of autonomy is the concept of personhood; in other words, what we mean by the idea of a 'person'. For Peter Singer to say that the word person is the same as human being is incorrect and is speciesist. Many animals have many of the criteria that we would associate with persons and some human beings do not have the criteria.

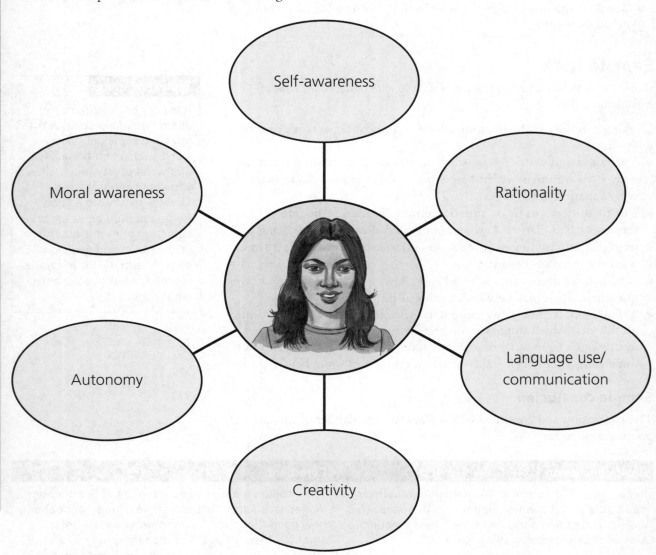

6 Business ethics

6.1 Introduction

REVISED

It is difficult to go very far without coming into contact with the topic of business ethics. Whenever we purchase goods online or in real life and whenever we step into our workplaces, we step into ethical issues, many of which may in fact be initially hidden. The topic of business ethics takes Milton Friedman's rejection of the idea of corporate social responsibility as its starting point. Some ethicists, however, think that businesses do have responsibilities; those who don't believe this may however value ethics as they believe that good ethics is good business. The topic also examines the impact of globalisation upon ethics as modern technology seems to present a whole range of new possibilities. In assessing each of these issues, the Kantian and utilitarian approaches to the topic will be examined.

The specification says

Topic	Content	Key knowledge
Business ethics	Key ideas, including: ● corporate social responsibility	What it is (that a business has responsibility towards the community and environment) and its application to stakeholders, such as employees, customers, the local community, the country as whole and governments
	● whistle-blowing	What it is (that an employee discloses wrongdoing to the employer or the public) and its application to the contract between employee and employer
	● good ethics is good business	What it is (that good business decisions are good ethical decisions) and its application to shareholders and profit-making
	● globalisation	What it is (that around the world economies, industries, markets, cultures and policy-making are integrated) and its impact on stakeholders
Learners should have the opportunity to discuss issues raised by these areas of business ethics, including: ● the application of Kantian ethics and utilitarianism to business ethics ● whether or not the concept of corporate social responsibility is nothing more than 'hypocritical window-dressing' covering the greed of a business intent on making profits ● whether or not human beings can flourish in the context of capitalism and consumerism ● whether globalisation encourages or discourages the pursuit of good ethics as the foundation of good business.		

6.2 Corporate social responsibility

One key debate in business ethics is around **corporate social responsibility**: the idea that businesses are not just there to make money but also have wider ethical responsibilities to all **stakeholders** and their wider community.

Challenging corporate social responsibility

The idea of corporate social responsibility was most famously challenged by economist Milton Friedman (1912–2006). Friedman's ideas have proved very influential in both the United Kingdom and the United States since the 1970s. He argues that whilst individuals in their own time may choose as persons to take on social responsibilities or do charitable things, as employees they must serve the corporation or company, and that company cannot have responsibilities. If the business makes money then **stockholders**, CEOs, etc., may decide to spend their money benefitting the community, but this is not a responsibility of the corporation. Likewise a free market may allow higher wages. If we want businesses to benefit society then we make them into public employees not private companies. Friedman argues that this involves an acceptance of **socialism** not capitalism.

> **Key quote**
>
> There is one and only one social responsibility of business – to use its resources and engage in activities designed to increase its profits so long as it stays within the rules of the game, which is to say, engages in open and free competition without deception or fraud.
>
> Friedman

What might corporate social responsibility involve?

Not everyone accepts Friedman's conclusions. There are good reasons for thinking that businesses do have responsibilities other than making money. Belief in corporate social responsibilities may be motivated by:
- a pragmatic approach that suggests 'good ethics is good business' (see Adam Smith)
- a Kantian sense of duty
- a religious sense of responsibility in how we treat humans and the rest of creation.

In the past, companies such as Cadbury built schools and parks for its workers; they believed that this was their duty towards their workers. Like many companies, it is keen to ensure its products are Fairtrade.

One example of an attempt to measure the extent to which companies display corporate social responsibility is the FTSE4Good index. Companies are given an ESG (environmental, social, governance) rating. The diagram on the next page indicates how companies might be measured.

> **Key quote**
>
> What does it mean to say that 'business' has responsibilities? Only people can have responsibilities. A corporation is an artificial person and in this sense may have artificial responsibilities, but 'business' as a whole cannot be said to have responsibilities, even in this vague sense.
>
> Friedman, *The Social Responsibility of Business Is to Increase its Profits*

> **Key words**
>
> **Corporate social responsibility** The idea that a business or organisation has ethical responsibilities to the wider community and environment
>
> **Stakeholder** Any individuals or groups who are affected by the actions of the business or organisation
>
> **Stockholder** The individuals who own the company or shares (shareholders) in the company and hence gain when the company profits
>
> **Socialism** A political and economic theory which argues that the means of production should be owned or regulated by the community as a whole

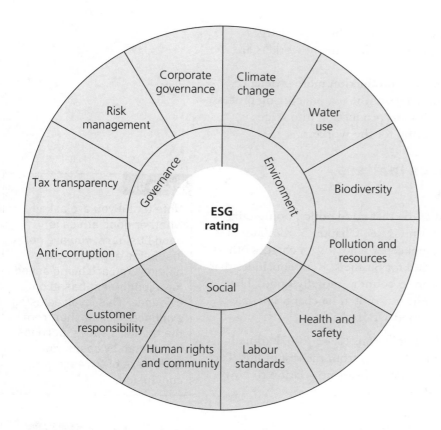

The model automatically excludes companies that are involved in weapons manufacture or production of tobacco.

Now test yourself

TESTED

1 What is corporate social responsibility?
2 Why does Friedman not believe in it?

6.3 Good ethics as good business

REVISED

As we saw in the previous section, Milton Friedman argues that good ethics may or may not be good business. Provided a business plays by the legal rules, it does not have to be ethical if this stands in the way of its profits.

Adam Smith: good ethics is good business

Adam Smith (1723–1790), one of the fathers of **capitalism**, takes a slightly softer view than Friedman. He shows that very often good ethics is good business. Smith's approach is essentially utilitarian.

Businesses have a symbiotic relationship with both their customers and their employees. Although it may benefit us in the short term to overcharge customers or pay low wages, we will ultimately harm our reputation and may make less money ultimately. Hence when we provide good service to others, Smith argues that we do so out of self-interest knowing that we will benefit in the end.

Nevertheless, Smith is primarily focused on how businesses can make money and two of his most famous ideas illustrate this.

Key word

Capitalism An economic system based on private ownership and free trade rather than government intervention

Key quote

It is not from the benevolence of the butcher, the brewer, or the baker that we expect our dinner, but from their regard to their own self-interest.

Smith, *The Wealth of Nations*

- The **law of supply and demand**: how much a business charges or how much it pays its workers is linked to how many workers are needed or are available.
- The **division of labour** makes factory production more efficient. Instead of one person doing all the stages of the manufacturing process, a 'conveyer belt'-type system which splits production into stages is more efficient, even if it is more boring for the workers.

Immanuel Kant: good ethics matters more than good business

Immanuel Kant (1724–1804) would argue that good ethics, doing our duty, is more important than good business (see Chapter 3, Kantian ethics). Kant uses the example of a shopkeeper who always charges others fairly because he knows that this is good for business. Kant concludes that even this is not sufficient for the action to count as morally good. The shopkeeper is acting in his own interest. It is only if he charges people fairly out of duty that this becomes a good action.

The modern American ethicist Robert Solomons (1942–2007) argued similarly that it is not possible to divide business from the rest of life. Too often people's behaviour in their business lives bears no relation to how they act outside of work. This should not be the case.

> **Exam tip**
>
> Note that if you are asked whether good ethics is good business, you are not just being asked for your opinion. You are being asked for a judgement based on evidence. This involves using evidence such as that from the thinkers above, perhaps illustrated by cases you are aware of to reach your conclusion.

Now test yourself

TESTED

3 In what way can Adam Smith's views be seen as broadly utilitarian?
4 Look at the VW emissions case (page 50). How would Friedman, Smith and Kant respond?

6.4 Whistleblowing

REVISED

The term **whistleblowing** refers to any situation where an employee, or in some cases other stakeholders, raises concerns of an ethical or legal nature about how an organisation is behaving. It is an ethical concern rather than a personal grievance. It differs from a normal concern in that they are likely to have gone above their immediate management or outside the organisation altogether.

> **Key word**
>
> **Whistleblowing** When an employee acts in the public interest to alert the employer or the public to wrongdoing within the organisation

Types of whistleblowing

Whistleblowing can be private or public.

- **Private**. The whistleblower raises concerns internally within the company in question. For example, a black teacher is given a written warning for having spoken to students inappropriately. He becomes aware that a white colleague who is also a senior manager received no punishment for a similar offence. A concerned colleague uses the college whistleblowing policy to raise this with governors as a case of racial discrimination.
- **Public**. The whistleblower raises concerns outside the organisation in question – for example, by alerting the media. For example, a hospital doctor is concerned that a new procedure introduced by managers is putting patients' lives at risk. Following failed attempts to explain the issue to managers and having seen an increase in patient deaths, she contacts the newspapers.

Why might someone become a whistleblower?

The following diagram illustrates some situations where whistleblowing may arise.

The cost of whistleblowing

Whistleblowers take a great risk in raising concerns, even though there are laws to protect whistleblowers, including anonymous procedures in some companies. In reality, they can face retaliation from colleagues, legal action and, in some cases, lose their job and future earnings. The 2015 'Freedom to Speak Out' report into NHS whistleblowing found that 30 per cent of whistleblowers felt unsafe and some had contemplated suicide.

Ethics and whistleblowing

In resorting to whistleblowing, an employee has to balance their loyalty to their company with any wider public issues and their need to live with their own conscience:

● Allowing whistleblowing ensures that companies take their corporate social responsibilities seriously. They know that there may be follow up if they behave unethically.
● Whistleblowing encourages integrity from employees. If I know that a colleague may report any over-claiming on expenses I am less likely to behave dishonestly.
● However, it can be argued that there are some situations where loyalty to the company is the most important thing. This is one reason why Edward Snowden's revelations about US intelligence were so controversial.
● In Kantian ethics, one must carry out one's duty as an employee; however, there are occasions when wider duties to our fellow human beings may override these.
● In some professions such as medicine and teaching, there are certain duties that are integral to the profession regardless of what an individual hospital or school may be saying.
● For utilitarians, whistleblowers have to make calculations about the greater good or harm that may come from choosing to speak out or to remain silent.

Now test yourself

TESTED ☐

5 What is meant by whistleblowing?

6.5 Globalisation and business

What is globalisation?

Globalisation refers to the integration of economies, trading and political movements around the world. On a simple understanding, we may say that 'the world is getting smaller'. Our ability to make connections is both quicker and more widespread than our ancestors, who would have done most business within their local town. Modern life has raised interesting possibilities.

- Technologically, we can communicate with all manner of people in various locations immediately.
- Politically and economically, countries are open to trade and very few countries have closed borders or are totally self-reliant: North Korea being one possible exception.
- Culturally, we are more connected. We are able to purchase the same brands wherever we are and are able to enjoy worldwide food in our own high streets.

Thanks to the power of the Internet, most of us have functioned as global traders!

> **Key word**
>
> **Globalisation** The integration of economies, industries, markets, culture and policy-making around the world

Effects of globalisation

Globalisation has produced a number of effects.

- The rise of larger multinational corporations with divisions in various countries.
- Increased competition in manufacturing and services – it is often possible to get things done cheaper in other countries.
- Lower wages or loss of jobs in developed countries such as the United Kingdom and the United States as manufacturing can be done more cheaply abroad.
- In developing countries, such as those in Africa and Asia, economic growth has been achieved as these countries are competitive economically.
- A loss of culture or national identity where global brands are seen on every high street.

Ethics and globalisation

Given that different countries have different health and safety requirements, government regulations and wages, globalisation enables businesses to 'shop around'. In the United Kingdom, we have a minimum wage and this leads some manufacturers to make products abroad. Manufacturers may be tempted to resort to the lowest common denominator and cut corners in terms of workers' rights in order to get products made cheaply (see, for example, the Rana Plaza Factory disaster, Bangladesh, in 2013).

A utilitarian may point to the benefits of globalisation as millions of people have been lifted out of poverty in countries such as China as a result of global trade. Yet not everyone wins as a result of globalisation; there is evidence that the gap between rich and poor is increasing. In addition, the utilitarian does not have a clear notion of rights and may see the greater good of globalisation as worth the price of some individual suffering.

A Kantian may be concerned that globalisation may increase the exploitation of persons in developing countries where multinationals dictate the terms of business. This may be seen almost as neo-colonialism, which may lead to a loss of identity in developing countries. Likewise in developed countries, jobs may be lost as things can be made more cheaply elsewhere.

A further issue on globalisation is the environment. There is little incentive to have rigorous environmental standards if the neighbouring country worries less about global warming. A country's president may then have to choose between enforcing environmental rules and losing business or reducing poverty in the country by relaxing environmental laws.

Now test yourself

TESTED ☐

6 Define globalisation.
7 What ethical issues may arise as a result of increased globalisation?

6.6 Utilitarianism and business

REVISED ☐

Utilitarianism is a popular theory to apply to business ethics as it seems to treat each situation differently.

Applying utilitarianism to business ethics

- An act utilitarian may make decisions on a case-by-case basis but a rule utilitarian may view that the long-term benefits of having a minimum wage or holiday entitlements may mean that a rule should be made on this issue regardless of individual cases.
- The value of 'utility' or usefulness means that utilitarianism is flexible as an ethical theory and weighs up individual situations considering economic benefits of the various options. In the words of Crane and Matten 'utilitarianism comes close to what we know as cost–benefit analysis' (Crane & Matten, *Business Ethics*, page 84).
- The classical utilitarians, Bentham and Mill, were very much in favour of freedom and minimal state intervention. This fits in well with Adam Smith's idea of enlightened self-interest. We should be free to run our businesses as we choose without interference, but we must bear in mind that behaving ethically may be the most profitable course of action in the long run.
- In cases involving whistleblowing, the utilitarian has to make a judgement regarding the risks and benefits for all concerned.
- The utilitarian could broadly support increased globalisation by pointing to the growth of economies in developing countries as a result of increased trade. However, this support would be on the assumption that the economic benefits are enjoyed by the majority of that country's citizens.

Case study

Volkswagen emissions

In 2014, VW was found to have fitted some of its cars with a device that enabled it to pass an exhaust emissions test; the car's on-board computer system would know that it was being tested and adjust the normal output. An act utilitarian might think this a very risky strategy; they would need to weigh up the options. If the device remained undetected then profits would be increased; however if, as actually happened, the deception was discovered, the cost of replacing cars, paying industry fines and long-term damage to reputation would count against such a course of action. Given the above, a rule utilitarian may think that honesty is almost always the best policy as the truth does tend to come out eventually. They may also argue that not all costs are financial and that environmental costs should have been considered.

Assessing utilitarianism on business ethics

Applying utilitarianism to business ethics raises a number of discussion points.

● Utilitarianism gives a significant amount of freedom: this leaves businesses free to consider situations for themselves and do what they calculate to be right.
● It can be argued that society flourishes best when lots of individuals flourish. This requires a variety of possible options rather than having rigorous rules imposed by governments.
● Utilitarianism depersonalises issues. This may be a good thing as it enables us to look logically rather than becoming emotionally attached. Alternatively this can mean that we consider numbers and profit before we consider people and their rights. Bentham famously described the idea of rights as 'nonsense on stilts'.
● One criticism of utilitarianism is that it is more difficult than it appears to be objective when weighing up the right course of action. We often see situations differently depending on our point of view.

> **Typical mistake**
>
> Candidates often claim that utilitarianism is selfish, but this is not the case. The utilitarian has to weigh up each situation as a genuine impartial observer.

Now test yourself

TESTED

8 Give one strength and one weakness of a utilitarian approach to business ethics.

6.7 Kantian ethics and business

REVISED

Kantian ethics is perhaps harder to apply to business than utilitarianism and is to some extent more demanding.

Applying Kantian ethics to business

● Kantian ethics states that we should do our duty regardless of our inclination or possible consequences. This includes possible loss of profit. In Kant's shopkeeper example (page 46), the shopkeeper would have been required to be honest even if this was not good for business.
● Kantian ethics also has implications for the employee. It challenges the widespread culture of over-claiming on expenses or using company items for personal business. Not only do employees have a duty of honesty towards their employers, it is not possible to universalise these dishonest actions.
● The requirement to treat persons as ends is very powerful. This leads to the idea of rights within the workplace and for consumers. It also leads

to the ideas of giving autonomy and dignity in the workplace. This can be used to argue that excessive and intrusive monitoring of workers would be morally wrong (see Case study below). Treating persons as ends would apply to all stakeholders in a business, including customers.

● Kantian ethics would most likely be supportive of whistleblowing where there are significant ethical concerns. Although employees have a duty to their company, they also have wider ethical responsibilities.

Case study

Sports Direct

In 2016, following an undercover investigation prompted by whistleblowers, a committee of MPs published a report criticising Sports Direct.

Workers were disciplined for being off sick, were timed on toilet breaks and made to queue unpaid to be body searched before leaving work. The MPs said that workers were 'being treated like commodities' (objects).

Assessing Kantian ethics on business

Applying Kantian ethics raises a number of points that are worth discussing.

● The theory gives priority to rights over profits. This is at first glance a good thing but it is debatable whether it is always realistic to ignore profits.

● Kantian ethics has a helpful focus on treating persons as ends.

● Universal law does not seem to give much help. This is because it is trying to do something that business does not do. Businesses make specific decisions in specific situations.

● Kantian ethics focuses on motive and the idea of doing the right thing for the right reason. However, motives are hard to assess. Who knows the real reason why the shopkeeper in Kant's own example is behaving honestly?

● The idea of duties to all the various stakeholders is fine in theory, but in practice may lead to conflicting duties. We may not be able to satisfy everyone. Friedman's idea that we should just focus on profit is at least clearer.

Exam tip

When assessing an ethical theory's approach to an issue as we are doing on this page, look at the general strengths and weaknesses of the theory and ask yourself if they apply to this topic. Try to find examples and think the issues through in advance.

Now test yourself

TESTED

9 Give one strength and one weakness of a Kantian approach to business ethics.

6.8 Assessing the issues

REVISED

Question: Is corporate social responsibility genuine?

Some businesses are genuine in their ethical actions and their whole business model is based on ethical concerns. However, for other businesses, there is an element of calculation in their actions. Good ethics leads to good publicity, which in turn is good for business. Several perspectives might be relevant in determining whether this is hypocritical.

- Utilitarians might approve of this calculation. The motive does not matter but money is made and good deeds are done so everyone wins.
- Kantians would want the motive to be genuine. If the action is not genuinely motivated then it is not truly good.
- Friedman would see the debate as irrelevant. There are no social responsibilities. If a business chooses to do ethically good actions because it leads to greater profits, this is fine, but it has no obligation to do so.

Question: Does globalisation encourage or discourage ethical business?

Most multinational corporations value their reputations and have very strong ethical statements on their websites and some – for example, Microsoft, who have donated over $1 billion to charity – back this up by their actions. In other cases, there is a concern that actions do not back up the fine words.

- Globalisation means global competition and this pressure to cut costs can mean a 'race to the bottom' in terms of wages and rights. Labour often goes to those who pay least and care least about rights.
- A utilitarian might point to generally increased living standards in developing countries as a result of globalisation. However, there are winners and losers in each country.
- A Kantian may be concerned that globalisation has increased the possibility of workers being mistreated in the pursuit of profit. However, this has always gone on to some extent and modern communication technology at least means that this may come to light more quickly.

Question: Can humans flourish in a capitalist culture?

Capitalism is based on private ownership and free trade; people flourish when they pursue their own desires within a free marketplace. It is not for the government to intervene to help failing businesses or to give overly complicated employment laws. These conditions sort themselves out as a business that is run badly or pays employees poorly either corrects this or goes out of business. This leads to some observations.

- Not all can flourish. The system is based on competition and there have to be winners and losers.
- Capitalism seems to positively encourage individualism, self-interest and **consumerism**.
- Karl Marx (1818–1883) famously criticised the capitalism of his day after seeing rich factory owners oppressing their workers. To make an excessive profit is effectively theft. If the worker's efforts create £200 worth of product but she is only paid £50 for the day and the rest goes to the business owner as profit, this is unfair.
- In modern times, socialists argue that privatisation means that profits are put above providing a quality service. This has been a criticism of several railway companies.
- In Kantian ethics, it could be argued that the word 'consumer' implies a means to an end relationship – likewise the phrase 'human resources' in employment rather than personnel may convey something about how we think of our employees.

Key quote

There are no values, no 'social' responsibilities in any sense other than the shared values and responsibilities of individuals. Society is a collection of individuals and of the various groups they voluntarily form.

Friedman

Key word

Consumerism A belief in the importance of acquiring material things

6.9 Summary and exam tips

Exam checklist

- Explain the idea of corporate social responsibility.
- Explain with examples the idea of whistleblowing.
- Explain the idea that good ethics is also good business.
- Explain what is meant by globalisation and how this is linked to this topic.
- Explain and assess how well the theory of utilitarianism addresses the issues in business ethics.
- Explain and assess how well the theory of Kantian ethics addresses the issues in business ethics.
- Assess whether corporate social responsibility is genuine or whether businesses are merely going through the ethical motions.
- Assess whether globalisation encourages or discourages businesses to be ethical.
- Consider whether humans can flourish in our capitalist consumerist society.

Sample work

Be careful when you are using examples to illustrate an answer, as you may find yourself doing on answers in this topic. It is important to ensure that examples are sufficient to support the point you are making but don't spend too much time describing cases – remember that most of the marks are for presenting an overall argument.

> **Exam tip**
>
> Obviously, there is no easy right or wrong answer to the issues in this chapter. For each of them you need to think carefully and use the evidence you have gained from studying the topic to argue your case.

Mainly descriptive example on whistleblowing	Example used to reinforce explanation or develop the argument
One example of private whistleblowing was the story of Barclays chief executive Jes Staley. He attempted to find out the identity of an individual who had written to the bank's board complaining about his actions in appointing someone he knew to a senior position. This is an example of private whistleblowing as the letter went to the bank's board and not outside to organisations such as the media.	One concern that a utilitarian may have with regard to whistleblowing is whether it is worth the risk in reporting unethical activity. In one recent case, the chief executive of Barclays Bank attempted to find out the identity of a whistleblower. This shows the risks that whistleblowers undertake which from a utilitarian point of view need to be balanced against possible gains.

> **Revision activity**
>
> Follow the business feed of a news website such as the BBC. When ethical stories arise (and they will), practise explaining the issues to others and explaining how utilitarians and Kantians may respond. Teaching others is often a great way of seeing if you have understood something.

Going further: Useful work or useless toil?

In a famous essay, the Victorian writer William Morris observed that there were two kinds of work: useful work and useless toil. Morris suggested that there were three things that made work useful: these were the hope of rest, hope of product (that a useful end product is produced) and the hope of finding pleasure in the work itself. This essay, intended as a challenge to some Victorian working practices, may still be relevant today and, although not directly influenced, is linked to Kant's idea of treating persons as ends.

7 Meta-ethical theories

7.1 Introduction

What is 'goodness?' What do people mean when they use this and other similar words? Do 'goodness' and 'right' and 'wrong' actually exist or is it all a matter of opinion? These questions are at the heart of the topic of **meta-ethics**. The topic analyses three main meta-ethical positions. Naturalism believes that right and wrong can be known empirically and that these truths reveal absolute moral standards. Intuitionism agrees with naturalism that there is such a thing as right and wrong yet disagrees on how it is known; for the intuitionist moral truths are self-evident, we 'just know'. Emotivism offers a different view to the previous two theories in arguing that there are no moral facts but that our ethical judgements are merely showing approval or disapproval, indicating subjective feelings on the issues. It argues that ethical claims are factually meaningless. Meta-ethics differs from **normative ethics**: normative ethical theories, such as utilitarianism, are a little like the tactics used to play the game of ethics. Meta-ethics asks questions about the game itself.

> **Key words**
>
> **Meta-ethics** From the Greek *meta* meaning above and beyond. The study of the meaning of ethical concepts
>
> **Normative ethics** Theories of ethics that give advice on how we ought to behave

The specification says

Topic	Content	Key knowledge
Meta-ethical theories	Naturalism	What it is (the belief that values can be defined in terms of some natural property in the world) and its application to absolutism
	Intuitionism	What it is (the belief that basic moral truths are indefinable but self-evident) and its application to the term 'good'
	Emotivism	What it is (the belief that ethical terms evince approval or disapproval) and its application to relativism

	Learners should have the opportunity to discuss issues related to meta-ethics, including:
	● whether or not what is meant by the word 'good' is the defining question in the study of ethics
	● whether or not ethical terms such as good, bad, right and wrong:
	  – have an objective factual basis that makes them true or false in describing something
	  – reflect only what is in the mind of the person using such terms
	  – can be said to be meaningful or meaningless
	● whether or not, from a common sense approach, people just know within themselves what is good, bad, right and wrong.	

7.2 Ethical naturalism

What is ethical naturalism?

Ethical **naturalism** believes that moral truths can be discovered by observation of the world. What is right and wrong can be established by looking at the world around us. It is a **moral realist** theory (believing that moral facts or truths actually exist) and is also **cognitivist**, believing that statements made about right and wrong are subject to being either true or false. Naturalists believe that ethical terms are meaningful.

Versions of ethical naturalism

There are different versions of ethical naturalism, but it is worth restating that the key feature they all have in common is the idea that moral values can be defined and discovered by looking at some aspect of the world around us. They are known **empirically**.

1 Aquinas (1224–1274) (see Chapter 1, Natural Law) would hold to a theological naturalism. The world has a God-given order built into it. Moral values can be worked out by understanding our God-given purpose and observing the natural order.

2 The British philosopher F.H. Bradley (1846–1924) argued that it is possible to understand our moral duties by observing our position or station in life. Although to some extent this is outdated and has a hint of Victorian class divisions, it could be argued that certain roles, for example, teacher, nurse, mother or brother, do seem to have certain duties or moral values attached to them.

3 Utilitarian thinkers, such as Bentham (1748–1832) and Mill (1806–1873), argue that we can discover right and wrong by discovering what actions lead to pleasure or pain. By observing that stabbing someone causes them pain, we can infer that this action is wrong.

Naturalism and absolutism

Ethical naturalism links very strongly with the idea of absolutism; however, they are not necessarily the same thing. One way of arguing for ethical naturalism is to use the thinking of Natural Law; the moral values that we discover when we consider purpose do indeed create absolute rules. Equally, there could be a utilitarian form of naturalism. However, if a thinker believes that right and wrong are linked to pleasure and pain, there may be more relative moral truths discovered.

An objection to naturalism

One objection to naturalism has its origins in the writings of David Hume and is known as the fact-value distinction or 'is–ought' problem. When we consider an action such as a murder we can describe the facts empirically – using statements involving the word 'is' – but we then move towards moral claims involving 'ought' and 'ought not'. Hume suggests that no matter how closely we examine the situation itself we will not be able to empirically see or hear the 'wrongness' of such an action.

> **Key words**
>
> **Naturalism** The idea that moral values can be correctly defined by observation of the natural world
>
> **Moral realism** The belief that right and wrong actually exist; they are real properties
>
> **Cognitivism** The belief that moral statements are subject to being either true or false

> **Key quote**
>
> What he has to do depends on what his place is, what his function is, and that all comes from his station in the organism.
>
> Bradley, *Ethical Studies*

> **Making links**
>
> Natural Law (Chapter 1) assumes naturalism to be the case and relies heavily on the idea that *telos* is built into the universe.

Now test yourself

1 What is meant by naturalism?

7.3 Intuitionism

What is intuitionism?

Intuitionism believes that moral truths can't be discovered by observation of the world. Right and wrong are not able to be defined, but are self-evident. We are able to know them by our intuition. Like naturalism, it is a moral realist theory, believing that moral facts or truths actually exist, and is also cognitivist, believing that statements made about right and wrong are subject to being either true or false (see Glossary for key words). Like naturalists, they believe that ethical terms are meaningful; however, they differ from naturalism regarding how moral values come to be known.

Moore's intuitionism

The most famous thinker to argue for intuitionism is G.E. Moore (1873–1958). The following is a summary of his views.

- Moore identifies the **naturalistic fallacy** as the key error that naturalism makes. For any natural property – for example, pleasure – we can still ask the question, 'Is pleasure really good?' The fact that it is possible to answer 'No' shows that pleasure (and other natural properties) are not the same as good.
- We don't recognise goodness through empirical facts; the 'good' is self-evident to our intuition.
- Moore uses the analogy with the colour yellow to explain how this intuition might work. If we were asked to describe yellow or present an argument that an object was yellow we would find the task difficult. We only answer the question of 'What is yellow?' by pointing to an object that is yellow. We are similarly able to recognise goodness. It cannot be defined but it can be shown and known.
- Moore explains the difference between simple and complex ideas: complex ideas – for example, a horse – are ideas that can be broken down into parts: the legs, the neck, etc. Simple ideas, such as the colour yellow, cannot be divided into parts. Moore states that goodness is a simple idea and simple ideas are grasped by intuition.

> **Key words**
>
> **Intuitionism** The idea that moral truths are indefinable and self-evident
>
> **Naturalistic fallacy** The idea that it is a mistake to define moral terms with reference to other non-moral or natural terms

> **Key quote**
>
> If I am asked, 'What is good?', my answer is that good is good, and that is the end of the matter. Or if I am asked, 'How is good to be defined?' my answer is that it cannot be defined, and that is all I have to say about it.
>
> G.E. Moore, *Principia Ethica*

> **Typical mistake**
>
> Note that intuitionism does not think that right and wrong depend on our personal intuition or feelings. The 'good' is a real thing and we are able to intuitively recognise it.

Assessing intuitionism: Do people just know what is right and wrong?

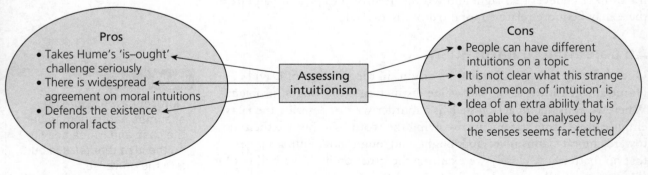

Pros
- Takes Hume's 'is–ought' challenge seriously
- There is widespread agreement on moral intuitions
- Defends the existence of moral facts

Assessing intuitionism

Cons
- People can have different intuitions on a topic
- It is not clear what this strange phenomenon of 'intuition' is
- Idea of an extra ability that is not able to be analysed by the senses seems far-fetched

Now test yourself

2 What is intuitionism?
3 Give one similarity and one difference between naturalism and intuitionism?

7.4 Emotivism

What is emotivism?

Emotivism believes that there are no moral truths; moral statements are based on feelings of approval or disapproval. It is an anti-realist theory, believing that there are no moral facts. It is also a **non-cognitivist** theory – believing that statements made about right and wrong are not subject to truth or falsity. The emotivist believes that ethical statements are meaningless.

The Vienna Circle and the verification principle

The background to emotivism is found in the work of the **logical positivists** and the philosophy of Hume.

The verification principle put forward by the logical positivists suggests that statements are only meaningful if (1) they are analytic statements (true by definition) or (2) they are synthetic statements that are verified by the senses. Hume had previously argued that moral judgements were feelings or sentiments rather than factual judgements. When we observe the facts of a situation we are not able to see the rightness or wrongness.

Ayer's emotivism

A.J. Ayer (1910–1989) agreed with the logical positivists on the verification principle. His weak version of it says that we should only view statements as meaningful if we are able to say how we could verify them (see the Philosophy of Religion section of the specification). As moral statements are neither logical nor provable by the senses, this means that they are factually meaningless.

Ayer argues that it is important to look at what ethical statements are for rather than look for 'meaning'. This means that we need to look at how speakers use the words 'right' and 'wrong'. Ethical statements show emotional states or feelings about issues. The words 'right' and 'wrong' don't add anything; they merely convey an approving or disapproving tone.

> **Key quote**
>
> The presence of an ethical symbol in a proposition adds nothing to its factual content. Thus if I say to someone, 'You acted wrongly in stealing that money,' I am not saying anything more than if I had simply said, 'You stole that money.' In adding that *this action is wrong*, I am not making any further statement about it. I am simply evincing my moral disapproval of it. It is as if I had said, 'You stole that money,' in a peculiar tone of horror, or written it with the addition of some special exclamation marks.
>
> A.J. Ayer, *Language, Truth and Logic*

Evince

Ayer uses the term 'evince' to explain how ethical statements may show an emotional state. It does not quite mean the same as expressing an emotional state, as Ayer points out that we may or may not actually feel the emotion that our words indicate.

> **Making links**
>
> The discussion as to whether ethical language is meaningful is parallel to the discussion of the meaningfulness of religious language in philosophy of religion (see the Philosophy of Religion book, Chapter 8).

> **Key quote**
>
> The vice entirely escapes you, as long as you consider the object.
>
> Hume, *A Treatise of Human Nature*

> **Key words**
>
> **Emotivism** The idea that moral statements are not statements of fact, but are indicators of emotional states
>
> **Non-cognitivism** The belief that moral statements are not subject to truth or falsity
>
> **Logical positivism** An idea developed by members of the Vienna Circle which considered philosophical analysis to be the way to determine whether an idea is meaningful

> **Now test yourself**
>
> TESTED
>
> 4 How does emotivism make use of the verification principle?

7.5 Ethical terms as objective and meaningful

In suggesting that ethical language may be objective and meaningful, we are claiming that our language is describing real facts when we use the terms 'good', 'bad', 'right' and 'wrong'. This page shows some of the arguments for and against naturalism and intuitionism – two theories that would support this view.

Arguing for and against moral facts (moral realism)

The following arguments apply to both naturalism and intuitionism.

- **Shared moral values**: Supporters of moral realism point to the broad agreement on moral values. Almost everyone would argue that torture, rape or unprovoked killing is wrong. Our agreement suggests that morality cannot just be a matter of personal opinion. However, it is possible to suggest that the glass is half empty rather than half full. There is significant cultural variation in morality, and issues, such as abortion, show that there isn't always a consensus.
- **Moral progress**: We have made considerable progress in our attitude to topics such as slavery and racism. This implies that our ethical language does describe real things. If there was no such thing as right and wrong then it would be impossible to talk of moral progress; progress requires a fixed end point to measure against. Without an actual right and wrong our twenty-first century attitudes are just different not better.
- **The need for a standard**: If there is no objective right and wrong then there can be no absolute standards. Although we currently believe in rights, tolerance and fairness, there is no reason why we couldn't change these beliefs and no reason why these values are better than hatred, racism and cannibalism. This seems a rather uncomfortable place to be but is a logical consequence if values really are a matter of opinion.

Difficulties for naturalism

In addition to the points above, there are specific difficulties for the naturalist position (see also page 55).

- Some naturalists rely on the idea of there being a purpose or *telos* built into the universe. This is challenged by various thinkers, including evolutionists and existentialists, who reject the idea of purpose (see Chapter 1 on Natural Law).
- Hume identifies the gap between factual 'is' statements and value judgements 'ought' and 'ought not'. Moral judgements are primarily a matter of emotion, nothing factual can be observed that leads to ideas of right and wrong (page 55).
- Moore shows that there is a naturalistic fallacy, particularly if we claim that pleasure is good (see page 56).

Arguing for and against intuitionism

The following arguments are specific to intuitionism. It is worth noting that although intuitionists see morality as absolute and objective they do not base moral values on 'facts' in the empirical sense.

- The advantage of intuitionism over naturalism is that it seems to avoid problems such as the is–ought gap and the naturalistic fallacy, yet still presents morality as objective.
- One difficulty with intuitionism is that people's intuitions often seem to differ. The reply to this difficulty given by one intuitionist, H.A. Pritchard, is that some people have better intuition than others. This may not seem very convincing.

7.6 Ethical terms as subjective or meaningless

In suggesting that ethical language may be subjective and meaningless, we are claiming that our language is not describing real facts when we use the terms 'good', 'bad', 'right' and 'wrong'. Instead, it is merely reflecting what is in our minds rather than describing the world. Hence this page shows some of the arguments for and against emotivism. It is worth noting that in some cases they will be the opposite of the arguments found on the previous page.

Arguing for and against morality as subjective and meaningless (moral anti-realism)

The following arguments are covered in more detail on the previous page.

- *Lack of shared moral values*: The supporter of emotivism points to the differences in moral values and behaviour rather than the similarities.
- *Moral progress*: It is difficult for those who do not believe in moral values to properly explain moral progress.
- *The need for a standard*: For emotivists and other anti-realists, the lack of overall standards is a problem. They attempt to answer this by appealing to the good sense of human beings; although there is no objective and absolute right and wrong, we are able to have subjective agreement on what good moral standards are.
- If morality is subjective and not based on facts then the difficulties of the naturalistic fallacy and the is–ought gap are avoided.

In addition, the following arguments are also relevant.

- *Trivialisation*: Theories such as emotivism which argue that ethics is subjective and meaningless trivialise ethics. If morality is just personal preference then 'I don't like killing' becomes no more important than 'I prefer the red sweets'.
- *No discussion*: A key criticism of emotivism is that it prevents intelligent and reasoned discussion. For example, our discussion of an issue such as abortion is reduced to a shouting match of 'abortion, boo!' versus 'abortion, hurray!'

> **Key word**
>
> **Moral anti-realism** The belief that right and wrong do not actually exist; ethics is a matter of opinion

Going further: Prescriptivism and error theory

It is possible to be sympathetic to Ayer's basic idea that there are no objective moral facts but feel that Ayer's emotivism leaves a lot to be desired. Two other theories that offer subjective views of moral statements are Hare's prescriptivism and Mackie's error theory

1 **Prescriptivism**: R.M. Hare (1919–2002) argues that when we make moral statements we are not just expressing feelings, we are prescribing those views to others. To say that 'killing is wrong' is to effectively say 'I do not approve of killing and you should not do so either.' In making moral statements, we are attempting to give imperatives to others.

2 **Error Theory**: J.L. Mackie (1917–1981) argues that there are no moral facts, merely subjective values. However, when we make moral statements, we speak as though the statements we make are actually true or false. We are in error. A belief in objective values is built into moral language, but this belief is false. Within everyday life, we assume and speak in terms of moral facts, yet when viewed objectively from the outside these facts do not exist.

> **Now test yourself**
>
> 5 What is the 'naturalistic fallacy'?
> 6 Which of the three meta-ethical theories believes that ethical language is meaningless?
>
> TESTED

7.7 Is 'What is good?' the key question in ethics?

The layers of ethics

> **Meta ethics**: From the Greek *meta* meaning above and beyond. The study of the meaning of ethical concepts, e.g. what does 'good' mean? Does it actually exist?

> **Normative ethics**: Considers ethical theories that give advice on how we ought to behave, e.g. utilitarianism, Natural Law

> **Applied ethics**: Discusses specific problems in ethics, e.g. should euthanasia be permitted?

> **Descriptive ethics**: Explores different ethical views that vary across cultures – such as the sociological study of ethics

'What is good?' *is* the key question in ethics

In taking this position, we would be arguing that the meta-ethical question is the most relevant question in ethics and forms the basis of other questions.

- The levels of questioning suggested in the diagram above show that it is the meta-ethical question that needs addressing first. If we are unclear on what goodness is, it is difficult to build normative theories on how we should act.
- Related to this, the word 'good' may mean very different things. If we each mean something different by the word, e.g. pleasure, an intuition or a feeling, then practical discussions in ethics become tricky.
- Addressing what goodness is also affects our moral motivations. If I believe that the universe has fixed God-given standards of goodness then I will be more inclined to be good than if I think that goodness is just a subjective idea.

'What is good?' is *not* the key question in ethics

In taking this position, we would be arguing that the meta-ethical question is not the most relevant question as either there are no objective moral truths or the question itself cannot be answered.

- The meta-ethical question of what goodness is, is a remote and complex question. There seems to be little agreement on what the answer might be. It also seems to bear little relation to the practical issues in ethics.
- Regardless of whether we answer the question of what goodness is, we are not excused from the practicalities of needing to make ethical decisions about the issues we face. 'What shall I do?' seems a far more pressing question and this would point us towards theories such as utilitarianism or Kantian ethics rather than meta-ethics.

Now test yourself

7 What is meant by normative ethics?
8 Why might meta-ethics be seen as more important than normative ethics?

Exam checklist

- Explain and assess ethical naturalism.
- Explain and assess intuitionism.
- Explain and assess emotivism.
- Explain what is meant by meta-ethics and consider whether the meta-ethical question 'What is good?' is the key question in ethics.
- Assess whether ethical terms (good, bad, right, wrong) are objective facts.
- Assess whether ethical terms (good, bad, right, wrong) are meaningful or meaningless.

Sample work

Exam tip

The topic of meta-ethics can fall prey to the general topic answer: sometimes less is more. There is a temptation to think that the examiner needs to see every theory and several thinkers on each theory. However, the mark scheme looks for depth and for good selection of material. There is a danger that a general topic answer may both lack depth and show poor selection. Be brave and leave some things out in order to go into detail on the points that you include.

The examples below illustrate the point. The first example aims to cover all the weaknesses of intuitionism in one paragraph, whereas the second one is selective in covering one point and evaluative rather than just stating the material.

Example 1	Example 2
There are lots of weaknesses of intuitionism. It isn't clear what intuition is or where it is. Also intuitionists disagree with each other about what intuition shows. Ockham's Razor (the idea that we should always take the simplest explanation) would also suggest that intuition is unnecessary and doesn't add anything to our explanation. So intuitionism is not a successful theory.	Intuitionism also has a number of weaknesses. First, intuitionists often disagree with each other regarding the moral truths that may be discovered by our intuition. If intuition does give us moral truths that are not just a matter of opinion then it would seem strange that these would differ. In response to difficulties such as this, intuitionists such as Pritchard have argued that we all have different intuitions, although some of us are better at intuiting than others. Yet this seems to be a little evasive and doesn't really address the point.

Revision activity

Using the specification for this topic on page 54 and the checklist on this page, attempt to write three possible exam questions. Read your revision notes and then plan model answers. When you are feeling confident turn one of them into a full practice essay.

8 Conscience

8.1 Introduction

We all have a common sense understanding of the term 'conscience'. We may picture it as a gut instinct or inner voice that tells us what is right or wrong. Academic theories about what the conscience is are generally a little more developed than this and typically fall into one of two camps. There are those who argue that conscience is an actual thing that has some link to God, and there are those who wish to show that conscience is not a real thing in one sense but is actually the product of our own psychology. In terms of the specification, Aquinas' theological view of the conscience is the example of the former approach, and Freud's psychological view of the conscience illustrates the latter. This topic seeks to examine which view is closer to the truth about conscience.

The specification says

Topic	Content	Key knowledge
Conscience	Aquinas' theological approach	Details of this approach, including: • *ratio* (reason placed in every person as a result of being created in the image of God) • *synderesis* (inner principle directing a person towards good and away from evil) • *conscientia* (a person's reason making moral judgements) • vincible ignorance (lack of knowledge for which a person is responsible) • invincible ignorance (lack of knowledge for which a person is not responsible)
	Freud's psychological approach	Details of this approach, including: • psychosexual development (early childhood awareness of libido) • id (instinctive impulses that seek satisfaction in pleasure) • ego (mediates between the id and the demands of social interaction) • superego (contradicts the id and working on internalised ideals from parents and society tries to make the ego behave morally)

	Learners should have the opportunity to discuss issues related to ideas about conscience, including:
	• comparison between Aquinas and Freud:
	  – on the concept of guilt
	  – on the presence or absence of God within the workings of the conscience and superego
	  – on the process of moral decision-making
	• whether conscience is linked to, or separate from, reason and the unconscious mind
	• whether conscience exists at all or is instead an umbrella term covering various factors involved in moral decision-making, such as culture, environment, genetic predisposition and education.	

8.2 Aquinas on conscience – *synderesis* and *conscientia*

Aquinas' view of the conscience is unusual among theological views of the conscience in that the conscience is not a feeling or an inner voice but is rather the process of reasoning. It is the rational ability to understand the difference between right and wrong.

Reasoning and God

Aquinas uses the idea of right reason (or *recta ratio*). He believes that our ability to reason is given to us by God as a result of being created in the image of God. It then becomes our responsibility to use our God-given reasoning correctly. We do this by developing the intellectual virtue of prudence or *phronesis* – the ability to make judgements based on the circumstances we find ourselves in.

Synderesis and *conscientia*

For Aquinas, conscience is the 'mind of man making moral judgements'. It comes in two parts – **synderesis** and **conscientia**.

Synderesis is our natural inclination that we seek to 'do good and avoid evil'. It involves our awareness of what the moral rules are (see Chapter 1, Natural Law).

As the quote to the right shows, *synderesis* is not a one-off act but a habit of reasoning that we develop with practice so that we will come to understand and be able to apply the moral rules. One way of imagining this is to think of *synderesis* as a safe that we possess and developing our prudence/reasoning as acquiring the key.

Of course it is possible that we become confused as to what the good is and we seek an apparent good rather than a real good. We have a responsibility (1) to educate our conscience and become better at reasoning and thinking through the moral rules; (2) to develop our conscience through the repeated use of 'right reason'.

Conscientia is the practical outworking of *synderesis*. It is the intellectual process of making actual moral judgements and applying them to the situations that we face. Conscience is something that is an act. As Joseph Fletcher would later argue (see Chapter 2), conscience is a verb not a noun; this is certainly true of Aquinas' understanding of *conscientia*.

> **Key quote**
>
> Conscience is not a power, but an act … For conscience, according to the very nature of the word, implies the relation of knowledge to something … knowledge applied to an individual case.
>
> Aquinas, *Summa Theologica*

Now test yourself

1 What is *recta ratio*?
2 What are the two parts of Aquinas' theory of conscience?

> **Making links**
>
> You may wish to remind yourself of Aquinas' theory of Natural Law, particularly the *synderesis* rule and real and apparent goods, in preparation for this topic (page 4).

> **Key words**
>
> *Synderesis* The inner principle directing a person towards good and away from evil
>
> *Conscientia* A person's reason making moral judgements

> **Key quote**
>
> It is therefore clear that 'synderesis' is not a power, but a natural habit.
>
> Aquinas, *Summa Theologica*

8.3 Aquinas – vincible and invincible ignorance

In other theological views where God speaks to us or gives an infallible intuition, it is difficult to see how conscience could be mistaken. Aquinas, however, allows for this possibility. The errors of conscience can be explained by our ignorance.

Aquinas – conscience making mistakes

Conscience can make mistakes in a number of ways. It may be that we do not properly develop or educate our conscience yet we may also have difficulties in the '*conscientia*' – the actual application of moral rules. For example, we may know that it is wrong to steal but not think that copying a CD is an example of stealing. Aquinas believes that we develop our conscience as we gain more experience of reasoning and applying moral rules; hopefully we develop our **phronesis** or prudence so that we make fewer errors. In terms of the errors that we make Aquinas categorises them as showing either **vincible ignorance** or **invincible ignorance**. He uses an unusual and implausible example to illustrate his point:

Vincible ignorance involves a lack of knowledge for which the person is responsible. If a man sleeps with someone other than his wife because he is unaware of the moral rule about adultery or thinks that it does not apply in his case, he is responsible for his error. He ought to know the rule and not pursue an apparent good.

Invincible ignorance involves a lack of knowledge for which the person is not responsible. If a man knowing that adultery is wrong sleeps with a woman believing her to be his wife (and she believes him to be her husband!) then there is no wrongdoing, it is a genuine if unlikely mistake.

The authority of conscience

Whether our conscience is right or wrong, it is effectively all we have in the moment of decision, so Aquinas argues that we are obliged to follow our conscience. It carries authority even on the occasions that it is wrong.

Going further: An alternative theological view of conscience

An alternative theological view of the conscience is found in the writings of J.H. Newman (1801–1890). Unlike Aquinas, Newman's view of the conscience is more of an immediate inner voice rather than our own reasoning. Newman starts with our experience of conscience; he argues that it is a key part of our psychology in the same way as memory and imagination might be. Conscience is effectively God's voice speaking to us directly. It is authoritative and we ought to obey it. We experience guilt and shame when we disobey it.

> **Key words**
>
> **Phronesis** A practical wisdom, particularly in relation to moral decisions
>
> **Vincible ignorance** A lack of knowledge for which a person is responsible
>
> **Invincible ignorance** A lack of knowledge for which a person is not responsible

> **Typical mistake**
>
> Some candidates wrongly assume that Aquinas' view of the conscience is that it is God speaking to us – a little like the view given by Newman. However for Aquinas, conscience is more intellectual and rational. God does not speak to us through conscience; rather he has given us the tools to work out what we ought to do.

Now test yourself

3 What is the difference between a vincible ignorance and an invincible ignorance, according to Aquinas?
4 How does Aquinas' view of conscience differ from Newman's alternative theological view of conscience?

8.4 Freud's psychological view of conscience

Sigmund Freud (1856–1939) rejects the idea of God and the soul. The mind is like a machine and psychology is the process of scientifically studying and unpacking the layers of this complicated machine. For Freud the mind has three layers.

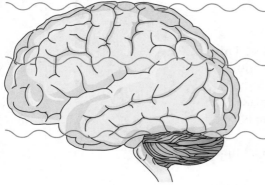

Consciousness
Those thoughts and desires that we can and do experience

Preconscious
Those thoughts and feelings that we aren't experiencing but may come to the surface at some point

Unconscious
The thoughts and feelings that are buried beneath the surface of our mind and cannot be retrieved, except by psychoanalysis

Freud on personality

Human personality is made up of three aspects.
1 The **ego** is the conscious self, the part seen by the outside world and the thinking that we are most conscious of.
2 The **id** is the unconscious self which contains basic desires and drives – two key ones being sex and death! The ego is our reasoning but the id is our basic drives and passions. Superego is something that is within the ego – it is a reaction to the id.
3 The **superego** is a set of moral controls and ideas given by authority and often opposed by the id. Freud is particularly interested in the superego (which he calls ego-ideal in his earlier books).

Forming the superego and guilt

For Freud, conscience is superego and can be explained psychologically. It is formed by society, particularly parents. It is a reaction to all the demands that are placed upon a person that they cannot live up to. We start to internalise the voice of our parents but this continues with every interaction with authority figures. A gap emerges between the ego (who we actually are) and the demands of the superego (our idea of an ideal person formed by all these early interactions).

Guilt occurs when we go against our conscience/superego.

The superego 'retains the character of the father' but as we get older other masters and authority figures are also significant.

Psychosexual development: the Oedipus complex

For Freud, all psychological problems are caused by sexuality, specifically early childhood awareness of libido. Freud argues that one further source of guilt is the Oedipus complex. A male child in its presexual development develops a fixation for his mother and perceives the father as an obstacle to the fulfilment of these sexual desires. The child has an ambivalent relationship to the father – he is fearful and jealous of the father, but eventually comes to identify with him and admire him. These feelings, which are repressed, cause guilt and shame. He speculates that female children develop the Electra complex, which is similar but involves female attraction to the father.

Key words

Ego Our conscious self that mediates between the id and the demands of social interaction

Id The instinctive impulses that seek satisfaction in pleasure

Superego The internalised ideals from parents and society that try to make the ego behave morally

---

Key quote

The ego ideal (superego), therefore, is the heir of the Oedipus complex and thus it is also the expression of the most powerful impulses … experienced by the libido in the Id.

Freud, *The Ego and the Id*

Now test yourself

5 What are the three aspects of human personality according to Freud?
6 How does the superego acquire its moral ideas?

TESTED

8.5 Assessing Aquinas' theological approach to conscience

Aquinas puts forward a view of the conscience that is dependent on reason. It does not see conscience as the product of the unconscious mind. He believes that conscience is a real thing that is given by God.

Supporting Aquinas' view

- Aquinas' view of the conscience is rational rather than intuitive. This can be seen as an improvement on other theological views as this requires reasoning rather than relying on 'gut instinct'.
- It explains that conscience can be mistaken and that we can make moral mistakes. This is more difficult for theories where there is a direct link to God.
- It explains how we come to change our minds on moral issues. Our conscience can be developed through education.
- It also explains moral disagreement, which is also a difficulty for those who believe God directly speaks through conscience. Surely if God had communicated, we would all agree on what the standards are.

Difficulties for Aquinas' view

- Aquinas' view does not fit with our experience of conscience feelings. Conscience does feel more intuitive and emotional in its promptings. We may rationalise at a later stage but the immediate experience is intuitive.
- Aquinas does not prioritise divine revelation; many Christians believe that God communicates directly, revealing his moral standards to us.
- Aquinas doesn't take into account the social and environmental factors that inevitably seem to affect our moral views. Freud seems to be right to suggest that these are a factor.

Exam tip

Remember that in order to access higher levels on the mark scheme, points such as those on this page need developing and discussing, not just stating. There is an example below.

Developing an argument

Point	Development/discussion
One difficulty facing Aquinas' view of the conscience is that there is a tension between his view that conscience can make mistakes and that you should always obey your conscience. It would seem that an erring conscience should not be taken as authoritative.	One response that Aquinas might make to this issue is to point out that your conscience is the main source of moral guidance that you have and if you have been responsible in educating your conscience then the best that you can do is to follow it. Indeed the very process of reasoning about our actions is a process of conscience. It would be strange if at the end of that process we were to reject our own conclusions.

Now test yourself

7 According to Aquinas, why does the conscience make mistakes?

8.6 Assessing conscience as psychological or from society

Freud puts forward a view of the conscience that sees it as the product of the unconscious mind. Hence, for Freud, conscience is not dependent on reason. It is not a real existing thing, but is an umbrella term covering various factors such as our upbringing and psychological development.

Supporting Freud's view

- Freud helpfully begins with our psychological experience of guilt and attempts to provide an explanation. This could be seen as a better starting point than that of Aquinas, who bypasses how we initially experience conscience.
- Freud sees his explanation of conscience and the discipline of psychology as scientific. He attempts to ground the explanation in empirical facts.
- There is some support for theories such as Freud's which attempt to show conscience is not a real thing but is more an umbrella term for various factors. Richard Dawkins has given an evolutionary account of how conscience could arise based on the idea that co-operation and treating others well would be a desirable trait and this trait would be passed on over many generations.
- Other psychologists, such as Piaget, do link morality and conscience with childhood development.

Difficulties with Freud's view

- Freud is atheistic and assumes a natural explanation of the phenomenon of guilt; however, it is possible that guilt could arise from a God-given instinct.
- Freud's view on morality which links our moral values to our upbringing would surely reveal more differences in moral values than there are. Moral values are largely shared regardless of culture and upbringing.
- Critics of Freud suggest that his research, although empirical, to some extent has limited support as ideas such as the Oedipus complex were based on a handful of case studies.
- A further issue with Freud's work on the unconscious is that his ideas cannot be falsified (proved right or wrong). This led the philosopher of science Karl Popper (1902–1994) to criticise Freud's work and to say that because of this Freudian psychoanalysis is not really science at all.
- It is possible to agree that Freud explains conscience in some individuals but that for others conscience functions in a better and higher way (see Fromm's alternative psychological account on page 69).

Making links

Look at the topic of falsification in the Philosophy of Religion book, Chapter 9. The same criticism made of religious belief is being applied here to Freud.

Exam tip

When developing an argument, make sure that points raised are discussed and analysed in order to access the higher levels of the mark scheme.

Now test yourself

8 How does Freud's view of conscience link to the idea of falsification?

TESTED

Point	Development/discussion
One key objection to Freud's view of the conscience is found in the idea of the Oedipus complex. Freud's idea is that one source of guilt is our early sexual urges for the parent of the opposite sex.	This is rejected by many psychologists and does not explain sources of guilt for those who have had a single parent or same-sex upbringing. In addition, Karl Popper rightly observes that like much of Freudian psychology, it is unfalsifiable. Yet in response to this objection, supporters of Freud may object that the Oedipus complex is not a key aspect of Freudian views on the conscience. The notion that we acquire irrational guilt from the standards of our parents and teachers survives without this much discredited idea. Hence this in itself would not automatically rule out Freud's view overall.

8.7 Comparing Aquinas and Freud

Specification point on conscience	What Aquinas says	What Freud says
Linked to reason	Yes	No
Product of unconscious mind	No	Yes
Whether conscience exists at all	Yes	No – just the name for a phenomenon
Conscience as an umbrella term for various factors such as culture, environment, genetics, education	No	Yes – particularly culture and environment

The concept of guilt

Freud and Aquinas seem to be starting at different points when it comes to the conscience. Freud starts with the feeling of guilt and seeks to explain it. Aquinas is not really interested in the psychological issues of guilt and responsibility.

Aquinas argues that the most important aspect of human beings is rationality so it is important to start with the process of reasoning. For Aquinas, guilt would merely be a byproduct of acting against the way your conscience directs you.

For Freud, conscience is guilt but not objective guilt. It is a psychological phenomenon that we might overcome as our guilt is not necessarily logical. For Aquinas, guilt is a logical feeling if we have reasoned correctly and then still acted against our conscience.

The presence or absence of God within conscience and/or superego

Aquinas sees our conscience as God-given, albeit indirectly as our reasoning is God-given. For Freud, God is a human invention; we create the idea of God to provide comfort when faced with a dangerous world where death may strike at any moment.

For Aquinas, God and religion bring humans wholeness. By following divine law and rightly reasoning, our conscience helps us to become better people. For Freud, religion based on the idea of God causes neuroses and prevents us from becoming psychologically whole.

Although Freud himself rules out God, this is not a necessary part of his theory. It may be that the superego he identifies is part of our God-given personality and moral framework. For Aquinas, God may not seem necessary, yet he is the one who creates humanity and provides the tool of conscience.

The process of moral decision making

For Aquinas, moral decision making is rational and involves decisions about what we believe God requires us to do. For Freud, moral decision making may be a reflection on the needs of the id and the superego, but often these are unconscious instincts rather than deliberately chosen thoughts.

For Freud, our moral thinking is learned and caused – it is not innate and it is not free. We cannot help these guilty feelings and where the gap between ego and superego is large we can develop psychological issues. However, although we are not obliged to follow the demands of conscience – our moral standards may be irrational. How good the contents of our superego are is dependent upon the quality of our upbringing.

Aquinas is not fully aware of developments in modern psychology and attempts to approach the issue theologically. He is aware that we have emotions and instincts but believes that these can be controlled by our more important side, the rational.

8.8 Summary and exam tips

REVISED

Exam checklist

- Explain Aquinas' view of the conscience, including ideas such as *ratio*, *synderesis*, *conscientia* and vincible/invincible ignorance.
- Explain Freud's view of the conscience, including ideas such as psychosexual development, ego, id and superego.
- Assess whether conscience is rational or a product of the unconscious mind.
- Assess whether conscience is produced by culture, upbringing and society.
- Critically compare Aquinas and Freud's views of the conscience, including the role of God.

Going further: Fromm's alternative psychological explanation

Erich Fromm (1900–1980) partially agrees with Freud's view of the conscience. He believes that each of us has two consciences: the authoritarian conscience and the humanistic conscience. Which one of these is stronger depends on the individual and their personality.

1 **The authoritarian conscience**: Like Freud, this conscience begins with a fear of authority. We internalise our feelings of fear so that our inner voice becomes that of the authority. We fear and obey the authority's rules even when they are absent. A good authoritarian conscience gives us a sense of wellbeing and security as we trust the authority to look after us. In a bad authoritarian conscience, such as possessed by many of the Nazis, obedience becomes the supreme moral value and fear of punishment overrides all other feelings.

2 **The humanistic conscience**: The humanistic conscience differs greatly from Freudian views. It is our own inner voice reacting to how well we are functioning in life. It is a reaction of ourselves to our own behaviour, almost like looking in a mirror and asking, 'What sort of person am I?' Fromm argues that this conscience is a higher and more developed conscience and he regrets that for many of us, this conscience is drowned out by the louder authoritarian conscience.

Exam tip

It is potentially risky bringing in a different thinker who isn't named in the specification in your answer. Whether this is irrelevance or an intelligent extended discussion depends on how material is treated. If the material is not linked to the question carefully then it is irrelevant, no matter how well you explain it. If it is clearly linked – for example, Fromm is used to critically assess Freud – then it can show high-level understanding of the topic and clear evaluation of the issues. Often it is not what you use but how you use it that secures the marks.

Exam tip

You may be asked to 'critically compare' the views of Aquinas and Freud on aspects of the conscience. The previous section enables you to do the compare and contrast. You will need to reflect on who you think has the better view and argue for it. That is the 'critical' aspect of the comparison.

9 Sexual ethics

9.1 Introduction

The topic of sex and relationships is an important feature of modern life and often dominates the media. However, the discussion of sexual ethics is often less developed. Attitudes to topics such as homosexuality, premarital sex and extramarital sex have changed greatly and at first glance seem to be moving from a predominantly religious view to a more secular one. This topic looks at these three issues as examples of topics within sexual ethics and applies the ideas of the ethical theories studied in this unit. Two of the theories are religious: Natural Law and situation ethics; whereas the other two theories are secular: utilitarianism and Kantian ethics. In addition to considering how helpful these theories may be, this topic reflects on whether religious ideas continue to be useful in sexual ethics and whether ethical theories have any value at all in making decisions about something that is so personal and private.

The specification says

Topic	Content	Key knowledge
Sexual ethics	Consideration of the following areas of sexual ethics: ● premarital and extramarital sex ● homosexuality	
	The influence of developments in religious beliefs and practices on debates about the morality, legality and tolerability of these areas of sexual ethics	Traditional religious beliefs and practices (from any religious perspectives) regarding these areas of sexual ethics How these beliefs and practices have changed over time, including: ● key teachings influencing these beliefs and practices ● the ideas of religious figures and institutions
	Application of the following theories to these areas of sexual ethics: ● Natural Law ● situation ethics ● Kantian ethics ● utilitarianism	The impact of secularism on these areas of sexual ethics: ● how these theories might be used to make moral decisions in these areas of sexual ethics ● issues raised in the application of these theories
	Learners should have the opportunity to discuss issues related to ideas about sexual ethics and changing attitudes towards it, including: ● whether or not religious beliefs and practices concerning sex and relationships have a continuing role in the area of sexual ethics ● whether choices in the area of sexual behaviour should be entirely private and personal, or whether they should be subject to societal norms and legislation ● whether normative theories are useful in what they might say about sexual ethics.	

9.2 Premarital and extramarital sex

In Christianity, there has traditionally been a strong link between sex and marriage; hence in order to consider **premarital** and **extramarital sex**, it is important to first examine ideas about marriage.

Religion and marriage

The idea of marriage has been found in almost all human societies in some form or other. In Christian thought, a marriage has the following elements:

- It is a public event where commitment is declared and promises are made.
- It is intended for companionship, raising of children and the fulfilment of sexual desire.
- It is intended to be a lifelong relationship 'til death do us part'.
- It is a **covenant** relationship where from that day onwards the two individuals are one in mind and body. For Catholic Christians, marriage is regarded as one of the **sacraments**.

Issues around premarital sex

In considering issues around premarital sex, it is worth recognising that the phrase premarital sex covers a range of possibilities, from someone who engages in casual sexual encounters with a variety of partners right through to a couple who have faithfully cohabited for many years but have chosen not to marry. Modern attitudes to premarital sex have been affected by a number of factors.

- **Cohabitation**: There has been an increase in cohabiting couples. In the 1960s, only 5% of couples cohabited. It is now at least 50%. Couples cohabit for a variety of reasons: they may be living together as a 'trial' before marriage, they may be cohabiting as an alternative to marriage, or they may be opposed to the idea of marriage.
- **Contraception**: Contraception is now available more freely than in previous generations. Hence people can be sexually active with a relatively low risk of pregnancy or sexually transmitted diseases.
- **Secularisation**: The idea that sex should not occur outside marriage was largely influenced by religious teaching; these teachings are now less prominent in people's lives. Cohabitation is no longer referred to as 'living in sin'.

Issues around extramarital sex

Religious teaching on extramarital sex is seemingly clearer than the teaching on premarital sex. 'Do not commit adultery' is one of the Ten Commandments and Jesus' teaching on divorce in one of the gospels states that divorce is only permissible when **adultery** has occurred. Yet a number of issues arise.

- Is extramarital sex still morally wrong if the couple in question has an agreement to have an open marriage?
- If a person who is in a committed cohabiting relationship has an affair, is this premarital or extramarital sex? Is it as wrong as a married person having an affair?
- Religious teaching on monogamous marriage has gradually evolved. In the Old Testament, Abraham had a concubine as well as a wife; David and Solomon had multiple wives.

Key words

Premarital sex Sex before marriage

Extramarital sex Sex outside of marriage where at least one party is married to someone else, adultery

Covenant A sacred agreement between God and his people or between people in the sight of God

Sacrament An outward sign that is a means of receiving God's grace. Baptism and Eucharist are also sacraments

Key quote

That is why a man leaves his father and mother and is united to his wife and they become one flesh.
Genesis 2:24

Key word

Adultery Sexual intercourse between a married person and someone who is not their spouse

Now test yourself

1 What is important about marriage according to Christians?

TESTED

9.3 Homosexuality

REVISED

The law on homosexuality

The law on rights for gay people has changed considerably over the last 60 years.

- The 1957 Wolfenden Report recommended that homosexual acts between consenting adults should not be illegal. This recommendation was supported by an appeal to Mill's Harm Principle (see quote).
- The Hart-Devlin debate in the 1960s saw two leading law lords disagree on the recommendation. Patrick Devlin argued that **homosexuality** should remain illegal as this is part of society's common morality and society needs a common morality to survive. Herbert Hart disagreed, believing that society should only enforce a 'minimal morality' in order to prevent harm to others.
- Hart's argument won the day and homosexual acts between consenting adults were decriminalised in 1967.
- In 2005, gay people were allowed to undertake civil partnerships. Full marriage rights were given in 2014.

In addition to the legislation around homosexuality, there has been a shift socially in terms of attitudes towards homosexuality.

Religion and homosexuality

Much of the Biblical material that opposes homosexuality comes from the Old Testament.

- In *Leviticus* 18:22, it commands that men should 'not have sexual relations with a man as one does with a woman'. Later on, it suggests that such an act is punishable by death.
- The city of Sodom is destroyed by God in the book of *Genesis* and one of its crimes seems to be homosexual acts between men.
- The text to the right from 1 *Corinthians* 6 indicates that there is also some opposition to homosexuality in the New Testament.

It is a matter of debate and Biblical interpretation as to whether these texts are held to apply to Christians today or reflect the culture and time in which they were written.

For Christians following a Natural Law ethic, the primary precept of reproduction governs much of their thinking on sexual ethics and would seem to rule out homosexual relationships.

Issues around homosexuality

In discussing the topic of homosexuality, particularly with the link to religious teaching, it is important to consider the wider issues; it is not just about the rights and wrongs of gay sex. These issues may include:

- The distinction between act and inclination: are gay Christians required to be celibate?
- Is gay marriage really a marriage in the spiritual sense and should churches allow (or be forced to hold) gay weddings?
- The adoption of children by gay couples.
- The ordination of gay clergy.
- Issues around toleration and free speech: if a sincerely held religious view opposes homosexuality how can it be expressed?
- Can homosexuality be 'cured'? Controversial gay therapy courses are offered in some churches.

Key word

Homosexuality Sexual orientation or attraction to people of the same sex

---

Key quote

That the only purpose for which power can be rightfully exercised over any member of a civilized community, against his will, is to prevent harm to others. His own good, either physical or moral, is not a sufficient warrant.

J.S. Mill, *On Liberty*

Key quote

Neither the sexually immoral nor idolaters, nor adulterers, nor men who have sex with men ... will inherit the Kingdom of God.

1 *Corinthians* 6:9–10

Making links

This topic raises issues around Biblical interpretation and how the Bible is used for ethics. See Christian moral principles in the Developments in Christian Thought book, Chapter 5.

Now test yourself

2 Why might some Christians oppose gay marriage on ethical grounds?

TESTED

9.4 Considering Natural Law

There are two main religious theories that can be applied to sexual ethics. The first, Natural Law, takes an absolutist approach and tends to form a key part of Catholic ethics. It typically opposes premarital sex, extramarital sex and homosexuality.

Applying Natural Law

Natural Law has at its centre a concern for human flourishing. It holds that certain goods are required for human flourishing; to fulfil our *telos* or purpose is ultimately what is best for us. Aquinas' version of Natural Law holds that the primary precepts, including reproduction, are key to this human flourishing.

1 **Reproduction**: The idea that the *telos* or purpose of the sexual act, and one of our purposes as human beings is reproduction is central to Natural Law's rejection of homosexuality.
2 **Marriage**: Natural Law stresses the importance of marriage; it is a secondary precept that can be deduced as it brings order to society. Catholic morality has built upon this to suggest that sexual intercourse belongs only within marriage and that all sexual acts must be open to the possibility of procreation (see quote above). Children need the order and stability that a married relationship brings.
3 **Divine Law**: In addition to the point above on marriage, Natural Law also gives importance to the Divine Law revealed in scripture. 'Do not commit adultery' is one of the Ten Commandments and this would be sufficient to rule out extramarital sex even without the primary and secondary precepts.
4 **Real and apparent goods**: Although sex may lead to pleasure, the purpose of sex is reproduction. To pursue pleasure through premarital sex, extramarital sex or a homosexual relationship is an apparent good. Right reasoning about our *telos* would lead us to reject these ideas according to Natural Law.

Assessing Natural Law

In assessing Natural Law we might consider the following points.
- The focus on reproduction and preserving life is a good thing and prevents us from assuming a casual view of sex.
- Natural Law is linked to belief in God and is based on human reasoning. However, it is possible to debate the benefit of these links.
- Natural Law makes an assumption about the purpose of sex. Sexual relationships may equally have other purposes, such as being unitive or bringing pleasure.
- The idea of doing what is natural has been used to imply that homosexuality is unnatural, yet this cannot be the case if homosexual inclinations are part of people's nature.
- Natural Law is legalistic in its approach and has not kept pace with modern technological developments, for example, contraception and IVF. Sex does not have to be linked to reproduction and it is possible for gay couples to have children.

> **Key quote**
>
> The Church, nevertheless, in urging men to the observance of the precepts of the Natural Law, which it interprets by its constant doctrine, teaches that each and every marital act must of necessity retain its intrinsic relationship to the procreation of human life.
>
> Pope Paul VI, *Humanae Vitae*, 1968

> **Making links**
>
> Review the topic of Natural Law (Chapter 1) to remind yourself of the key ideas in this theory.

Now test yourself

TESTED

3 What is the main reason that Natural Law ethics opposes gay sex?

9.5 Considering situation ethics

The second religious ethical theory is situation ethics. It is a relativist and teleological ethical theory and tends to be adopted by liberal protestant Christians. It is supportive of premarital sex and homosexuality dependent on the context and can in extreme situations even support extramarital sex.

Applying situation ethics

Situation ethics according to Joseph Fletcher aims to provide a middle ground between religious legalistic attitudes and modern secular antinomianism. It has one key principle of doing the most loving thing in each situation.

1 **Agape**: Agape is described as unconditional love for one's neighbour. It is not to be confused with *eros*, which is sexual love, although in relationships it may be difficult to completely separate the two. In terms of premarital sex, Fletcher may draw a distinction between casual and promiscuous sex and sex within the context of a loving relationship.

2 **Criticism of religious ethics**: Fletcher is highly critical of religious theories based on Natural Law. He believed that this was particularly evident in terms of issues such as homosexuality. It is difficult to see how rejection of homosexuality can be the most loving thing to do.

3 **Extramarital sex**: Although it is harder to justify extramarital sex as the most loving thing, it is not impossible if an extreme situation presents itself. The case given in the key quote box is one where Fletcher, although not giving a definitive answer, may regard extramarital sex as acceptable.

4 **People centred**: Key to all of Fletcher's thinking are the ideas of relativism and personalism. What is right depends on the situation and on what is best for people; people are more important than rules.

Assessing situation ethics

In assessing situation ethics, the following points could be made.

● Situation ethics is helpful in drawing a distinction between casual or loveless sex and sex within a loving relationship. This is something that Natural Law, with its focus on rules, and utilitarianism, with its focus on pleasure, fail to achieve.

● Sexual ethics involves persons; hence it is right to look for a person-centred solution, such as situation ethics.

● Situation ethics overlooks religious commandments on sexuality, specifically 'do not commit adultery'. This is too flexible for some Christians and ignores the belief that such commands are revealed by God.

● Situation ethics seems to mainly focus on the most loving thing for those immediately involved in the situation. It needs to consider also the other people involved – for example, the effects on children or wider family.

● Situation ethics may be more helpful in extreme cases than in the everyday case. In most ordinary cases, there needs to be a clearer rule to follow.

> **Key quote**
>
> The defence agency wanted her to take a secretary's job in a Western European city; and under that cover 'involve' a married man who was working for a rival power ... When she protested that she couldn't put her personal integrity on the block, as sex for hire, they would only say 'It's like your brother risking his life or limb in Korea. We are sure this job can't be done any other way.'
>
> Fletcher, *Situation Ethics*

9.6 Do religious views still have a role in modern sexual ethics?

In terms of Western attitudes to sexuality, religious views, particularly those of Christianity, have been highly influential. In an increasingly secular society, should these views continue to have influence?

Religion as a negative force with no continuing role in sexual ethics

The case for rejecting a continuing role for religion is as follows:

- Attitudes to homosexuality within conservative religious countries lead to persecution of gay people. Our own liberal and tolerant society has evolved beyond that way of thinking.
- Attitudes to the role of women are also outdated. J.S. Mill (1806–1873) believed that the traditional Christian view of marriage subjugated women and gave them a lesser role.
- Narrow Natural Law views which link sex to reproduction both devalue the potential unitive elements of sex and, through lack of contraception, risk producing overly large families.
- The French philosopher Michael Foucault (1926–1984) argued that religion is responsible for a key error in sexual ethics – the idea that some things are normal and other things are abnormal. We are no longer required to look at the world through this unhelpful lens.

Religion as a positive force that has a continuing role in sexual ethics

The case for a continuing role for religion is as follows:

- If we are to understand the context of religious views, we will see that both Christianity and Islam gave women more rights than they enjoyed in first-century Palestine or pre-Islamic Arabia, respectively. In addition many of the aspects of sexual ethics that we may criticise as religious are in fact not religious but cultural.
- A religious ethic may offer a valuable caution against a modern liberal culture where sexual ethics has no real rules other than consent. A Christian attitude to sex prevents the sexual act being cheapened and stresses the unitive aspect of sexual intercourse.
- There is some evidence that marriage is linked to happiness and better educational outcomes for children.

> **Exam tip**
>
> Look at the strengths and weaknesses of Natural Law and situation ethics on pages 73 and 74. These can be used to answer a question like the one earlier in this section.

Developing a more nuanced conclusion on religion

It may be that a more nuanced conclusion is called for to the question in this section. The following may be ideas worth exploring.

- Christianity and religion in general is too mixed a phenomenon to give a definitive answer. Natural Law and situation ethics, both religious approaches, are different. There are also literal and more liberal interpretations of Biblical material. There is also a development from polygamy in the Old Testament to monogamy in the time of Jesus.
- It could be argued that Christianity provided a useful framework in the past, securing rights for women and bringing stability to society. However, society no longer requires this framework as we are able to do this without religion.
- The perspective of Christianity can still be seen as one useful voice, but it is no longer the authoritative voice that it used to be.

> **Now test yourself**
>
> 4 Give one reason why religious views on sexual ethics may be seen as unhelpful in the modern day.
> 5 Give one reason why religious views may be seen as helpful in the modern day.
>
> TESTED

9.7 Considering utilitarianism

There are two main non-religious theories that can be applied to sexual ethics. The first is utilitarianism. This takes a relativist and teleological view of sexual ethics which, with the exception of rule utilitarianism, judges issues of premarital sex, extramarital sex and homosexuality on a case-by-case basis.

Applying utilitarianism

Utilitarianism is committed to providing the greatest balance of good over evil that is possible.

1 **Pleasure**. At first glance, Bentham's utilitarianism is straightforward as it is focused on pleasure; provided that the pleasure outweighs the pain, an action is a good action. This makes utilitarianism fairly liberal in its approach, would seem to permit most cases of premarital sex and would treat homosexual relationships the same as heterosexual ones.

2 **Tolerance**. Although Mill regards sexual pleasure as a lower pleasure (which may suggest that the relationship becomes the most important thing), his non-harm principle that a government should only intervene if others are being harmed suggests that differing sexual behaviours should be permitted. Mill might, as a rule utilitarian, also be able to allow premarital sex and homosexuality as no-one else is harmed. This principle might also provide grounds for opposing extramarital sex.

3 **Consent and preference**. Linked to the above, Peter Singer's preference utilitarianism argues that respect for the different preferences of persons is the most important consideration in determining overall happiness. It is not for us to express a view on the preferences of others unless those choices are directly causing us unhappiness. If I am homophobic, it is none of my business what the gay couple next door are doing. However, if I am the victim of my partner's affair then that may be a different matter. Rational consent is important to utilitarians.

4 **Evidence**. Utilitarians do not have a philosophical position on marriage versus cohabitation or heterosexuality versus homosexuality, but in aiming to achieve the greatest good for the greatest number, they are open to possible evidence. Recent reports suggesting that married couples are happier and healthier, and that the children of married parents do better statistically at school would be interesting to a utilitarian. If, and it is a big if, the evidence stands then they might adjust their views on the issues accordingly.

Assessing utilitarianism

In assessing utilitarianism, the following points could be made.

- Utilitarianism is progressive and modern. It is not dependent on outdated religious ideas, unlike Natural Law. Mill's non-harm principle played a key role in gay rights legislation.
- In a topic such as sexual ethics where situations are both private and varied, utilitarianism is a helpful, flexible approach.
- Bentham's utilitarianism focuses too much on majority pleasure. One famous criticism is that at least in theory Bentham could support gang rape. Bentham himself, as well as supporting homosexuality, also thought that pederasty – an older man having a sexual relationship with a young adolescent boy – was acceptable. Later versions of utilitarianism are less subject to these problems due to Mill's non-harm principle and his lesser focus on physical pleasure.

- If suffering and pain includes moral outrage then there would be a case for banning homosexuality. However, this would be what Mill refers to as the tyranny of the majority – where a majority imposes its view forcibly on a minority.
- In some cases, it requires assessment of the future; whether or not it is good to have an affair seems to be dependent on whether it is found out.

9.8 Considering Kantian ethics

REVISED

The second non-religious theory applied to sexual ethics is Kantian ethics. This theory takes an absolutist and deontological approach to issues in sexual ethics. It seeks to find rules that can be universalised and enable us to treat persons with dignity and value.

Applying Kantian ethics

Kantian ethics focuses on fulfilling one's rational duties. The keys to understanding what our duty is in different situations are the tests for the categorical imperative, particularly the idea of universalising rules and ensuring that persons are treated with dignity and respect.

1 The ideas of freedom and autonomy mean that rational consent is important to Kantian ethics. In addition treating someone as an end entails treating them with dignity; it could be argued that any sexual relationship that is totally driven by lust risks viewing the partner purely as an object.
2 **On homosexuality**: Kant himself disapproved of homosexuality, although this is not necessarily a logical consequence of his theory. While it is true that homosexuality cannot be universalised as the human race would die out, the requirement to treat people as ends would seem to suggest that gay people ought to be free to express this aspect of their identity.
3 **Marriage**: Kant holds a high view of marriage. It is a contract where persons give each other rights so that any sexual relationship that follows does not 'degrade human nature' by treating the other person as an object. This would rule out premarital sex, although it may be possible to argue that this is not necessarily a logical conclusion of the two tests.
4 **Extramarital sex**: In addition to the above, extramarital sex is ruled out by several other considerations: it breaks the promises made in marriage and Kant strongly opposes promise breaking, it treats at least one of the parties as a means to an end and it would be difficult to universalise extramarital sex without making marriage meaningless.

Assessing Kantian ethics

In assessing Kantian ethics, the following points could be made.
- The requirement that persons are respected is a useful insight and prevents a casual attitude to sex and the people involved.
- It is a secular theory, which may prove attractive in a less religious age.
- Kantian ethics is logical whereas often our feelings about sexual ethics are driven by emotion and personal bias. Kant's logic can be a good thing as it gives us a way of rationally analysing our feelings. However, it also makes Kantian ethics a cold and remote solution to issues.
- The universalisation test is not necessarily helpful as dilemmas in sexual ethics and the people involved are too varied for a universal rule.

Exam tip

In assessing an ethical theory such as utilitarianism or Kantian ethics on sexual ethics, look at the general strengths and weaknesses of the theory (see Chapters 3 and 4) and ask yourself which of these could apply here.

Now test yourself

6 Why might a utilitarian oppose extramarital sex?
7 Why might a Kantian oppose extramarital sex?

TESTED

9.9 Is sexual behaviour private?

Sexual behaviour as a personal and private matter

One challenge to attempts to bring in ethical theories to the area of sexual behaviour is that sex is personal and private. It is argued that this makes sexuality different to other topics in ethics. Hence, provided that consent is present, there ought to be no other ethical constraints. This is known as the contractarian view of sex and it is quite prevalent in modern thought.

One key to this view is the non-harm principle of J.S. Mill and the idea that society should only enforce a minimal morality; we should only have laws about that which harms others. In this view, it would seem that all consensual sex is permissible.

Sex cannot be a totally private and personal matter

However, it can be argued that sex is never totally private and personal. There are at least two people involved in a sexual relationship; more in the case of extramarital sex. In some situations, individuals outside the relationship such as families and children can be affected. This leads some to argue that sex should indeed be subject to societal norms and legislation.

Ethical theory

A further concern might be raised by Fletcher's criticism of modern secular ethics as antinomian. A modern approach to sexual ethics would seem to remove the link between sex and love and hence cheapen sex.

Linked to this might be the Kantian perspective that if we were to have no sexual ethics and were to treat sexual ethics as a private matter, we may end up tolerating situations where we allow persons to be treated as a means to an end.

Feminism

Some feminist thinkers have made a different argument that some form of sexual ethics is needed. Feminists recognise that the balance of power may not always be equal in relationships. Although there is widespread access to birth control, which has removed the logical link between sex and reproduction, the gender imbalance is not totally redressed. Women still lag behind men in the workplace as they shoulder more of the childcare and take more career breaks. They are more likely than men to suffer domestic violence or revenge porn. This suggests that sex cannot be totally private and is an important area of ethics.

> **Making links**
>
> The issues raised by feminism may be developed by reference to the 'Gender, and theology' topic, in the Developments in Christian Thought book, Chapter 8.

> **Revision activity**
>
> Produce four mind maps, one for each of the ethical theories in this topic. A detailed mind map should include how the theory would approach premarital sex, extramarital sex and homosexuality. It should also include some strengths and weaknesses of the approach.

Now test yourself

8 How does the non-harm principle help to defend the idea that sexuality is private?

9 Why might a feminist think that a sexual ethic might be needed?

9.10 Summary and exam tips

Exam checklist

- Explain issues arising from premarital and extramarital sex.
- Explain some of the issues surrounding homosexuality.
- Explain how religious attitudes to sex and sexuality have developed and influenced thinking in this area.
- Explain how the four ethical theories (Natural Law, situation ethics, Kantian ethics, utilitarianism) can be applied to help make decisions regarding sexual ethics.
- Assess whether religious views still have a role in modern sexual ethics.
- Assess whether sexual behaviour is private or whether it is a matter for ethical and legal discussion.
- Consider the extent to which each of the ethical theories is helpful in its response to sexual ethics.

Typical mistake

Although general knowledge of sexual attitudes and some of the sociological explanations for this is part of the background for this topic, it would be wrong to make this the main focus of the essay. Keep in mind that you are answering an ethics paper and it is the ethical ideas that must be at the forefront.

Sample work

Exam tip

You will have a maximum of 40 minutes per essay – perhaps around 35 minutes in reality, if you have planned and thought about the actual question (rather than seen a key word and just started writing). Use the time effectively and ensure that you don't waste time and ink on unnecessary sections. This is particularly the case in the introduction where candidates often feel the need to supply biography and background detail.

Two sample introductions are given below.

Basic introduction	Improved introduction
Homosexuality is an important moral issue. Homosexuality was illegal in Britain until 1967. The Wolfenden report had recommended that homosexual acts between consenting adults be decriminalised. This led to the Hart-Devlin debate where the Law Lords were influenced by J.S. Mill's non-harm principle. J.S. Mill was a follower of Jeremy Bentham and wrote in his book, *On Liberty*, that the only power that governments should have is to prevent us harming each other. This applies to homosexuality. No one is being harmed if there is consent. One ethical theory ...	Homosexuality raises many ethical issues. It was decriminalised in 1967 following the Wolfenden report, which used J.S. Mill's non-harm principle to suggest that in consenting homosexual relationships no one is being harmed, hence this does not need to be a matter for the law. One ethical theory ...

Glossary

Absolutism In ethics, the idea that right and wrong is fixed at all times and for all people

Act utilitarianism The idea that we should always perform the act that leads to the greatest balance of good over evil

Active euthanasia A treatment is given that directly causes the death of the individual

Adultery Sexual intercourse between a married person and someone who is not their spouse

Agape Unconditional love

Antinomianism Literally meaning to have no laws at all (Greek *nomos* = law)

Assisted suicide A person who wishes to die is helped to die by another person. They may or may not have a serious or terminal illness

Autonomy Literally 'self-ruling', the belief that we are free and able to make our own decisions

Capitalism An economic system based on private ownership and free trade rather than government intervention

Categorical imperative An unconditional moral obligation that we are able to work out using reason

Cognitivism The belief that moral statements are subject to being either true or false

Conscientia A person's reason making moral judgements

Consequentialism The idea that right and wrong is based on the outcome or consequences of actions

Consumerism A belief in the importance of acquiring material things

Corporate social responsibility The idea that a business or organisation has ethical responsibilities to the wider community and environment

Covenant A sacred agreement between God and his people or between people in the sight of God

Deontological An ethic that is focused on the rightness or wrongness of the action itself

Duty The action that is morally required

Ego Our conscious self that mediates between the id and the demands of social interaction

Emotivism The idea that moral statements are not statements of fact, but are indicators of emotional states

Eudaimonia Flourishing and living well, the ultimate end that all actions should lead towards

Euthanasia Literally 'a good death' (from the Greek *Eu* meaning well or good and *Thanatos* meaning death)

Existentialism A school of philosophy that begins with human existence rather than human essence, it argues that humans are free and don't have a fixed nature

Extramarital sex Sex outside of marriage where at least one party is married to someone else, adultery

Globalisation The integration of economies, industries, markets, culture and policy-making around the world

Good will The only truly intrinsically good thing, having good motives and intentions

Hedonic calculus A system for working out the amount of pleasure or pain involved in a course of action

Homosexuality Sexual orientation or attraction to people of the same sex

Hypothetical imperative A moral obligation that is dependent upon desiring the goal in question

Id The instinctive impulses that seek satisfaction in pleasure

Intuitionism The idea that moral truths are indefinable and self-evident

Invincible ignorance A lack of knowledge for which a person is not responsible

Kingdom of ends A hypothetical or imaginary state where people always act according to the moral rules and treat others as ends

Legalism The idea that ethical decision making is by a system of laws

Logical positivism An idea developed by members of the Vienna Circle which considered philosophical analysis to be the way to determine whether an idea is meaningful

Maxim Another word for moral rules or principles. They are the things that we act upon

Meta-ethics From the Greek *meta* meaning above and beyond. The study of the meaning of ethical concepts

Moral anti-realism The belief that right and wrong do not actually exist; ethics is a matter of opinion

Moral realism The belief that right and wrong actually exist; they are real properties

Naturalism The idea that moral values can be correctly defined by observation of the natural world

Naturalistic fallacy The idea that it is a mistake to define moral terms with reference to other non-moral or natural terms

Non-cognitivism The belief that moral statements are not subject to truth or falsity

Non-voluntary euthanasia Where a severely or terminally ill person's life is ended without their consent, perhaps because they are unable to give consent

Normative ethics Theories of ethics that give advice on how we ought to behave

Passive euthanasia A treatment is withheld and this indirectly causes the death of the individual

Persons as ends The idea that human beings should be treated with dignity and respect, and not as mere objects

Phronesis A practical wisdom, particularly in relation to moral decisions

Postulates Things that have to be assumed or are a basis for reasoning. For Kant, free will, immorality and God have to be postulated in order for morality to make sense

Pragmatism A philosophical idea that suggests 'truth' should be understood in terms of what works

Premarital sex Sex before marriage

Quality of life The idea that life's value depends on certain attributes or goods, for example, happiness, autonomy

Relativism The idea that what is right or wrong is not fixed but is dependent on situation or culture

Rule utilitarianism The idea that we should always follow the rule that generally leads to the greatest balance of good over evil

Sacrament An outward sign that is a means of receiving God's grace. Baptism and Eucharist are also sacraments

Sanctity of life The idea that life is intrinsically sacred or valuable

Socialism A political and economic theory which argues that the means of production should be owned or regulated by the community as a whole

Stakeholder Any individuals or groups who are affected by the actions of the business or organisation

Stockholder The individuals who own the company or shares (shareholders) in the company and hence gain when the company profits

Suicide A person makes a voluntary choice and takes their own life

Summum bonum The highest good, where virtue is rewarded by happiness

Superego The internalised ideals from parents and society that try to make the ego behave morally

Synderesis The inner principle directing a person towards good and away from evil

Teleological The idea that goodness is determined by the outcome of actions

Telos Literally 'end' or 'purpose'. The idea that everything has a purpose or aim

Universal law The principle that we should only carry out those acts that we are able to will as a law for everyone at all times

Utilitarianism The ethical idea that we should always seek to achieve the greatest balance of good over evil

Utility The idea of 'usefulness' that we should do whatever is useful in increasing overall good and decreasing overall evil

Vincible ignorance A lack of knowledge for which a person is responsible

Voluntary euthanasia Where a person's life is ended at their own request. Usually this is done by another individual and is because of a terminal illness

Whistleblowing When an employee acts in the public interest to alert the employer or the public to wrongdoing within the organisation

Now test yourself – answers

Chapter 1 Natural Law

1 Aristotle believes that all things have a *telos* or purpose. It is good when things and people fulfil their purpose.

2 *Eudaimonia* means living well or flourishing. It can also be translated as happiness or fulfilment.

3 Natural Law enables us to reason about things that are not directly mentioned in the Bible. It is a lower level of law than Divine Law and its conclusions should not contradict scripture.

4 The laws that countries make are Human Laws; they are lower than Natural Law and Divine Law.

5 Reproduce, preserve innocent life, education, live in an ordered society, worship God.

6 There are various possible examples so the following is not a complete list: Reproduction – do not use contraception; Preserve innocent life – do not permit abortion; Education – allow each child to have free schooling; Live in an ordered society – those who are able to should work; Worship God – allow time off for religious holidays.

7 The doctrine of double effect allows an action that has two possible effects – one good and one bad – to take place if it is the good effect that is intended. An example may be carrying out an abortion in order to save a pregnant woman's life.

8 *Telos* assumes that we are created by a God who gives us purpose. *Telos* also commits the naturalistic fallacy.

Chapter 2 Situation ethics

1 Agape is an unconditional love for our fellow human beings. It is not to be confused with sexual love or friendship love.

2 Legalism – the overreliance on systems of laws, and antinomianism – the complete lack of laws, are at the two ends.

3 The working principles or assumptions are pragmatism, relativism, positivism and personalism.

4 He would argue that love and justice are the same thing if correctly interpreted.

5 Fletcher says this because he does not believe actions are absolutely right or wrong. It would depend on whether adultery led to a loving outcome or not in that case.

6 Fletcher argues that situation ethics is to be seen as a religious theory as love for your neighbour sums up Jesus' key commandment. Critics would argue that this over-simplifies Jesus' words and that other commandments, for example, the Ten Commandments, are being ignored.

7 Both theories are relativistic and teleological.

Chapter 3 Kantian ethics

1 Absolutist, deontological, secular.

2 He means that we should do what is morally required regardless of how we feel or what the consequences may be.

3 A categorical imperative applies at all times regardless of consequences whereas a hypothetical imperative depends upon whether we want the outcome or not.

4 The categorical imperative, as it is our moral duty to obey it.

5 Lying, committing suicide, and possibly killing and stealing are all things that could not be universalised.

6 We are required to tell the truth about the location of the victim.

7 The *summum bonum* that virtue or goodness is rewarded requires that a being exists who is able to ensure that justice occurs.

Chapter 4 Utilitarianism

1 The key idea is that we should achieve the greatest balance of good over evil or the greatest good for the greatest number.

2 It means that the theory is focused on the outcome of a situation.

3 It is the idea that we should aim to do actions that tend to increase happiness and decrease unhappiness.

4 Intensity, duration, certainty, propinquity, fecundity, purity and extent – of the pleasure and/or pain.

5 Reading a newspaper, organising a community event, attending philosophy class, attending a concert and chatting with a friend might all be higher pleasures. Eating cake, drinking beer and sleeping are lower pleasures.

6 An act utilitarian works on a case-by-case basis, whereas a rule utilitarian seeks to apply general

principles about what may lead to the greater good.

7 A utilitarian would suggest that it is permissible to blow up and kill Big Jake if this is what is needed to save more lives.

8 Utilitarianism is impartial, secular, focuses on happiness, is straightforward, progressive and democratic.

9 Utilitarianism finds it difficult to measure pleasure and pain, may harm minorities, can be seen as a swine ethic, focuses only on pleasure, and may depend on our point of view.

Chapter 5 Euthanasia

1 Euthanasia means gentle or easy death.

2 Active euthanasia is where something is done to directly cause the individual's death. Passive euthanasia is where treatment is withheld and this indirectly causes death.

3 This is where the individual in question is unable to make the choice as to whether their life should be ended, e.g. someone in a coma.

4 'God creating humans in his own image' (*Genesis* 1:27), 'You shall not murder' (*Exodus* 20:13) and 'The Lord gave and the Lord has taken away' (*Job* 1:21).

5 An ordinary means is a treatment or procedure that is not out of the ordinary or unnatural, e.g. food and water. An extraordinary means is something that is unnatural or out of the ordinary, e.g. a highly expensive experimental drug.

6 The reference to not harming a patient or giving a deadly drug seems to rule out the idea of doctors being involved in euthanasia.

7 Preserving innocent life and possibly the precepts on worshipping God and living in an ordered society.

8 Quality of life – it supports euthanasia where this is the most loving option. Life is not seen as intrinsically valuable.

9 The slippery slope argument is the concern that once a small step is taken towards permitting euthanasia, we will then inevitably slide towards a devaluing of life as a whole and this may include forced or pressurised euthanasia.

Chapter 6 Business ethics

1 Corporate social responsibility is the idea that a business has wider responsibilities to the community and environment; that the business is not just about making profits.

2 Friedman believes that only persons can have ethical responsibilities. Businesses are not persons.

3 Smith's view is that there is a greater good that can be achieved by treating others fairly.

4 Friedman might argue that Volkswagen has no responsibility to be truthful to customers, although if it were certain that the deception would be discovered and that business would suffer, that answer would change. Smith would probably reason on utilitarian grounds that the relationship between business and customer requires honesty (bad PR is bad business). Kant would argue that truthfulness is important even if money is lost as a result.

5 Whistleblowing is when an individual raises an ethical concern about an organisation on public interest grounds.

6 Globalisation is the integration of economies, markets, culture and policymaking around the world. Colloquially, it is the sense that the world is getting smaller.

7 Various possible answers: loss of cultural identity due to global brands, wages being suppressed due to competition, outsourcing to countries where pay or conditions are poorer.

8 Utilitarianism gives businesses freedom to act as they see fit rather than be tied by rules. On the other hand, utilitarians may be prone to ignore rights and fairness if the greater good demands it.

9 Kantian ethics values rights over profits and has a helpful focus on persons. On the other hand, the principle of universal law is not that helpful as businesses face specific circumstances and situations. There may also at times be conflicting duties.

Chapter 7 Meta-ethical theories

1 Naturalism is the idea that we can work out moral values by observation of the world.

2 Intuitionism is the idea that moral values cannot be observed in the world but are indefinable and self-evident.

3 Both naturalism and intuitionism believe that moral facts or truths actually exist. They differ in that naturalism argues that these facts are empirically discoverable, whereas intuitionism believes they are self-evident to our intuition.

4 Emotivism argues that because moral statements are neither tautologies nor able to be verified by experience, then they are factually meaningless. This follows the rule upon which the verification principle judges meaning.

5 The naturalistic fallacy is the idea that the naturalist makes a mistake in trying to define moral values in terms of non-moral terms or empirical facts.

6 Emotivism.

7 Normative ethics describes ethical theories that give rules on how we ought to behave.

8 It can be argued that the meta-ethical question is more important as it is a higher level of question. Whether right or wrong exists affects how we answer what is right or wrong in a given situation.

Chapter 8 Conscience

1 Right reason – actions are deemed by Aquinas to be good or bad depending on whether they follow what is reasonable.

2 Synderesis – the inner principle that enables us to know what is good, and conscientia – the application of the principle to a situation, the actual moral judgement.

3 Vincible ignorance is a lack of knowledge for which the person is responsible. Invincible ignorance is a lack of knowledge for which the person is not responsible.

4 Aquinas' view of the conscience is of a rational process, it is a reasoning tool given to us by God. Newman sees conscience as intuitive, it is as if God is speaking to us directly.

5 The id, the ego and the superego.

6 The superego internalises the moral standards of those in authority, particularly those of parents.

7 According to Aquinas, if the conscience makes mistakes it is because of human error, namely our failure to properly educate our conscience.

8 Because Freud focuses on the unconscious, his ideas are not testable and this fails the falsification test according to Popper. This means that Freudian psychology is not proper science.

Chapter 9 Sexual ethics

1 It is a public agreement or covenant before God, a lifelong commitment. Some Christians also see marriage as a sacrament.

2 Biblically, they may believe that marriage is between male and female. They may also, if influenced by Natural Law, oppose gay marriage as children cannot be produced.

3 It cannot lead to reproduction and reproduction is one of the primary precepts.

4 A number of answers are possible here, such as being out of step with current liberal and tolerant thinking, society is now more secular, and providing too narrow a view of the purpose of sex.

5 It may be possible to argue that religious views help us to avoid cheapening sex or that keeping sex within marriage generally produces better outcomes.

6 They would consider that in most cases more pain is caused by extramarital relationships than pleasure obtained.

7 They would argue both that universalisation of extramarital sex would lead to the promises of marriage becoming meaningless and that in having an affair, people are being treated as a means to an end.

8 The non-harm principle suggests that people should be allowed their own views and act as they see fit as long as no one is harmed. Otherwise people's sexual behaviour is no one else's concern.

9 A feminist may feel that society is unequal and that women need some protection in the area of sexual ethics given the gender imbalance.